DT
DS

DELTA TEACHER DEVELOPMENT S

Series editor: Sandy Millin

Overt Teaching

Putting learners at the centre of their learning discussion

David Byrne and Mark Heffernan

Overt Teaching: Putting learners at the centre of their learning discussion

Today we are going to:

Use this section

So that we can:

Thank some people

Thank you to Gill for giving us the encouragement and opportunity many moons ago to first talk about Overt Teaching.

Thank you to Jess R. for suggesting the "Today we are going to / so that we can" framework all those years ago. Genius!

Thank you to Sandy and Kate for helping us edit our ramblings.

Online materials accompanying this title can be found at www.deltapublishing.co.uk.

Download the free DELTA Augmented app onto your device

Start picture recognition and scan the **contents page**

Download files and use them now or save them for later

1st edition 1 5 4 3 2 1 | 2027 26 25 24 23
The last figure shown denotes the year of impression.

DELTA Publishing, 2023
www.deltapublishing.co.uk

Authors: David Byrne / Mark Heffernan
Series Editor: Sandy Millin
Project Manager: Kate Baade
Cover and layout: Eva Lettenmayer
Design: Datagroup int, Timisoara
Printing and binding: Elanders GmbH, Waiblingen

Printed in Germany
ISBN: 978-3-12-501689-7

From the authors

Looking back, there have been so many moments in my career that have gradually led me towards writing this book. When working as a manager, one of the most common conversations I used to have was teachers coming to me after an observation and saying 'You should have stayed until after the break - we did an amazing activity where everyone was up and moving around.'

Initially, I couldn't work out why this frustrated me. In itself, this is a completely normal reaction by a teacher who had planned a fun, engaging activity and wanted feedback on it. I know that in my career as a teacher, I had done the same many times. Gradually, however, I began to realise where my frustration stemmed from. In our industry, there tended to be a focus on task over achievement. Completing the task was the end in itself, as opposed to discussing what had been learnt.

I didn't want to see a task in which learners were just moving around, switching groups and working with realia for the sake of it; I wanted to see learners going into a task knowing why they were doing the task, what success looked like as a whole, what their individual success looked like. I wanted to see time dedicated to discussing success after the task. I wanted time given for learners to repeat the task and upgrade their language. I wanted more teachers coming into the staffroom talking about the successful reflection task they carried out and not the running dictation they did.

It was around this time that I was introduced to the work of John Hattie, whose research will feature in this book, and I was able to see clearly the true impact that these pre- and post-task discussions can have on learning. It was then that Mark and I began leading workshops on this topic, which eventually led to the writing of this book.

David Byrne

When I was a younger teacher, there was lots of discussion about the negotiated syllabus, the idea that we should discuss with our learners what they wanted to learn. I always thought this was a good idea, but it tended to end up with learners demanding increased grammar input. As I became a more experienced teacher, I realised that whilst learners may think they want to study grammar more, it wasn't necessarily going to help them improve their fluency or receptive abilities.

The fact is our learners don't necessarily have the learning skills or curriculum knowledge to be choosing what exactly they should be learning in class on a day-to-day basis. What I think we can achieve with a more overt approach is to give our learners better tools which they can then use to make better decisions about exactly what they need. In this way, a negotiated syllabus might actually be possible, because only if learners know why working on a particular skill is important, how it is important and where they might use it, will they have a reason to desire its inclusion in their lessons.

Through an overt method, we can bring the learners along with us and in turn be better guided by their own more informed learning needs.

Mark Heffernan

Contents

Contents

A

Introduction

We have always loved being in the staffroom. As a Director of Studies, David always maintained that his place was, for the most part, in the staffroom working with the teachers, with the idea that happy, supported, effective teachers lead to happy, supported, effective learners. Staffrooms can be entertaining places, they can be collaborative, they can be cathartic; you might find yourself having a debate about the accuracy of 'if I were you' compared to 'if I was you' or discussing an incredible fact you found out about a learner's culture; you can find teachers helping each other with last-minute planning or suggesting this coursebook or that resource book.

No staffroom is entirely the same but one commonality we've encountered in all the staffrooms we've been lucky enough to inhabit over the years is the variety of teachers and teaching styles that make up the room. We all have the same aim but approach it in a variety of ways. And what is this aim? To help our learners become more effective communicators of English. Teachers, especially English language teachers, did not get into this career for financial gain. Almost every teacher we have ever worked with would say they have their learners' best interests at heart, that they want to help their learners make progress.

We all have the same goal but the techniques and approaches we employ to achieve this goal can be very different. Is grammar input the key to communicative competency or should we instead focus on lexis? Should we present all our input first and then practise it, or should we help learners to notice gaps in their knowledge by setting a task first? Should we present language to our learners or help them to discover it within a text? For a new teacher coming into our industry, there are so many opinions and so much evidence to sift through, much of it anecdotal evidence or teachers' own experiential evidence, which while subjective, should nevertheless not be ignored.

The aim of this book is not to answer all the questions posed in the paragraphs above. It is not to dictate how a teacher should teach, but rather to embrace that diversity of teaching styles. Instead, this book will allow you to choose how best to teach your learners, which material to use, which warmers to choose, whether to focus on grammar, lexis or both. Those decisions are completely your own. This book aims to give you the tools you need to engage your learners in the discussion of their own learning around these teaching decisions.

We believe that whatever your approach to teaching, when it comes to discussing learning, there are two types of teachers: Overt Teachers, who discuss learning explicitly with their learners, and Covert Teachers, who focus on input and avoid discussions of learning. In the next section, we will examine both in more detail and suggest why you might want to move from being a more Covert Teacher to a more Overt Teacher. We will provide practical steps and ideas to help you to do this.

Before continuing, you may wish to assess your current position on the Overt Teaching spectrum with the questionnaire on the next page.

Reflection questionnaire: how much Overt Teaching do you do?

Use the questionnaire to reflect on each of the major areas of Overt Teaching. This will help you to decide which areas of the book you wish to focus your attention on. You can return to this questionnaire periodically to reflect on your development.

1. **Knowing why:**
   a. I make classroom management decisions (e.g. grouping, monitoring) but I don't know why I make them.
   b. I know why I make some classroom management decisions.
   c. I know why I make classroom management decisions, but I never communicate this to my learners.
   d. I know why I make classroom management decisions. I discuss my decisions with my learners so they understand my process.

2. **Setting aims and objectives:**
   a. I do not know the aims and objectives for my lessons.
   b. I know what I want to achieve in lessons but don't think in much detail about how.
   c. I have a clear real-life objective for each lesson, but I'm not always sure how I will achieve it.
   d. I have a clear real-life objective for every lesson, and I know how I will achieve it.

3. **Communicating aims and objectives:**
   a. I do not know how to communicate my aims and objectives to learners.
   b. I display the aims and objectives but do not discuss them.
   c. I tell learners what the aims and objectives are.
   d. I involve learners in a discussion about the aims and objectives.

4. **Discussing success:**
   a. I do not know what success looks like in most major speaking or writing tasks.
   b. I remind learners what language they should use before an activity.
   c. I tell learners what success looks like before an activity.
   d. I negotiate success criteria with learners before an activity.

5. **Feedback and repetition:**
   a. I do not give learners feedback after speaking and writing tasks.
   b. I give feedback after speaking and writing tasks. It usually focuses on error correction.
   c. I ensure learners know what they need to do to improve.
   d. I ensure learners know what they need to do to improve next time and make sure they have the opportunity to do so.

6. **Overtly discussing sub-skills (e.g. listening for gist, writing effective paragraphs):**
   a. I do not know how to talk about sub-skills with my learners.
   b. I practise sub-skills but I do not talk to my learners about them.
   c. I practise sub-skills but I am not sure how to discuss them with my learners.
   d. I develop sub-skills and discuss with my learners how they can apply the skills to their lives.

7. **Reflection:**
   a. I do not know how to encourage learners to reflect.
   b. My learners do not reflect on what they have learnt.
   c. My learners reflect on the language they have learnt in the lesson.
   d. My learners reflect on what they learnt in the lesson and how they can apply it outside the classroom.

ISBN: 978-3-12-501689-7

Interpreting your results

Your answers will help you to decide which sections of the book would be most useful to you.

a. In this area you are unaware of how best to overtly discuss the learning process. Part A of this book will give you the background knowledge you need while Part B will give you practical tasks to try out in your lessons.

b. In this area, you are a Covert Teacher. You have an awareness of this area but do not openly discuss it with your learners. Part A of this book will make the case for taking a more Overt Approach in this area and share the research that supports it.

c. In this area you have some background knowledge but are not sure how best to apply it. Part B of this book will give you tips and practical ideas on how best to apply Overt Teaching in your lessons.

d. In this area, you are already an Overt Teacher. For further tips and ideas, read Part B, especially the 'Take it further' sections. For tips and ideas on how to apply Overt Teaching to other contexts, check out Part C.

What is Covert Teaching?

In its simplest form, Covert Teaching is **not** discussing learning or the lesson with learners. It is the belief that the aim of a lesson and indeed the aim of the many tasks that make up a lesson are the domain of the teacher alone. The Covert Teacher does not discuss these aims in detail with their learners, they do not expect to be questioned as to the reason for an activity and they expect their learners to trust them and to follow the lesson blindly from one exercise to the next. The Covert Teacher is constantly chasing that *Ah-ha* moment at the end of the class where the intricate threads they have woven throughout the lesson come together for their learners. As a teacher this can be quite rewarding, but it is perhaps less so for the learners.

The Covert Teacher focuses on input (especially of language) as its own end, as opposed to discussing what has been learnt from that input. In a language class, the emphasis is on **covering** language as opposed to **discovering** if it has been learnt. When writing about the origins of Demand High teaching in 2014, Jim Scrivener wrote

> I am beginning to wonder if there is actually any real link between completion of tasks and learning – or if learners having fun with games and quizzes and running around is anything more than what it appears to be on the surface: having fun with games and quizzes and running around. The learning is incidental, random, unpredictable – and unaddressed.

We would add to this list that the learning is not just unaddressed but unknown. Unfortunately, this approach means Covert Teachers are making uninformed decisions, as they are unlikely to know the impact of their teaching overall or their input specifically.

As Hattie and Zierer say (2018, p3):

> When you walk into a classroom and say to yourself, "My job is to evaluate my impact," then learners are the major beneficiaries.

Without knowing and discussing our impact, teaching a language can become more like ticking off items on a long list of acquisition. This was something we were both guilty of when we first started teaching. In his early teaching years in Ireland, David was teaching a pre-intermediate (A2/B1) group and the phrase 'to be into' appeared in an audio. When one of the learners asked him what it meant, David was slightly shocked as it had come up the week before in a lesson on hobbies and interests and he had explained it then. He opened the question up to the rest of the class but nobody else knew. He said to the learners: 'But we covered this last week. Can nobody remember it?' His initial reaction was that his learners were at fault, that they were not revising or taking effective notes or even paying attention. In reality, some or all of the blame lay on his shoulders. He had covered the lexis during a lesson but had no idea what impact his explanation had had, if any.

Reflection

- What could David have done differently?
- What might you have done in David's situation?

Read on to check your ideas.

Here are some options David could have considered.

- He might have discussed with the learners whether *to be into (something)* was a key piece of lexis for them, and their lives.
- In the lesson, there had been a number of ways of discussing hobbies that you like or don't like. Perhaps some of the learners felt *to be into* was too colloquial for them or wouldn't be as understood as *to be interested in* in their contexts, and had therefore ignored it. The learners could have talked about which words or phrases they would use.
- He could have discussed with them how they might use this specific piece of lexis outside the classroom.
- He could have given learners the opportunity to use it again in a final activity at the end of the class and given feedback on whether or not it had been successfully used by his learners.

Had he carried out (some of) these discussions, David would have been better able to say how effective his teaching had been, how his learners had engaged with the lexis, and whether this piece of lexis was relevant for them and their lives. Without any of these discussions around learning, it was just another piece in a long list of language that had emerged during the lesson and in this instance had not been retained. While we acknowledge that there are many factors at play when it comes to retaining lexis such as the number of times the item has been encountered, the fact was that in his early years of teaching David was unaware of the impact of his teaching. In general, lexis was being encountered at best but rarely engaged with. His board was often full of new language that had emerged during the lesson and often it was dutifully written down by the learners but rarely discussed in any meaningful way.

Another example of Covert Teaching happened when we were working in a school in London. One of our co-teachers came out of a lesson visibly distressed and when Mark asked what had happened, the teacher replied that his lesson had failed completely. They sat down and discussed it; Mark asked how he knew it had gone badly, and if he had discussed the lesson with his learners. The teacher replied, 'No, I knew it was bad, I could see their faces. I didn't want to talk to them about it.' We can of course understand the teacher's point of view, but avoidance of this conversation means the teacher is depriving themselves of key evidence as to how the lesson really went. In a way, they are hiding potential news, whether good and bad, from themselves and choosing to judge the lesson based on their own perception without involving the other stakeholders, the learners. Leaving the lesson without this knowledge can lead to teachers making uninformed decisions in the following lessons.

Avoiding discussions like the ones in these two lessons means that the Covert Teacher is often quite uninformed about what learners take from their teaching. The teacher views lessons through a single lens, their own interpretation of events, and therefore makes uninformed judgements about the effectiveness of their lessons. We've all left lessons feeling that they went terribly, only to find out in the next lesson that the learners had actually fully grasped everything we had taught them. On the other hand, we've all left lessons that we felt were unsuccessful and it turned out we were right. The reality is that without measuring impact and discussing it with learners, teachers can never truly know how effective their teaching is.

In a covert classroom, it is not just the teacher who remains uninformed. Learners will make their own judgements on the success of the lesson. These may be based on how much they spoke, what they felt they learnt or how often their errors were corrected. Without actual evidence of attainment or discussions on learning, however, they have no real evidence as to what they have actually learnt. This can unfortunately lead to learners believing a lesson was unsuccessful and blaming themselves, the teacher or the school. Over the years as managers, we have often spoken to learners who said they had learnt nothing in their lesson or in a week or lessons. Our general belief is that it would be next to impossible for a learner to consistently attend lessons without learning anything at all, but the fact remained that these learners had come to this conclusion, and it was their firm belief that it was true. While the reality might be different, those learners had no evidence to the contrary because the impact of the lesson and the teaching had neither been measured nor discussed in an overt manner.

Covert aims

We believe that not knowing what has been learnt begins with not knowing what you were supposed to learn. After all, how can you measure your success if you don't know what you are trying to achieve? We mentioned above that a lack of discussion around aims and objectives is a key example of Covert Teaching. Sometimes this can be a conscious choice on the part of the teacher, as for many teachers it might not seem like a beneficial use of valuable lesson time. When discussing the importance of aims and objectives with our teaching teams and at conferences, we have noticed that teachers' attitudes to aims and objectives tend to fall into the three categories below:

1. I always have aims but I don't communicate them to my learners.
2. I put aims on the board and communicate them because I was told to.
3. I don't know what my aims are.

Category 1 is the Covert Teacher, who believes that knowing the goal of the lesson is the domain of the teacher alone. By not discussing the intended lesson aims and objective, learners are left uninformed as to the direction of the lesson.

Category 2 is what we would describe as being 'unintentionally covert'. Aims have been put onto the board and therefore communicated to learners, but they haven't been discussed overtly. A box has been ticked, but in reality the result is the same as if the aims had been hidden from the learners entirely. This situation often comes about because well-meaning managers or accreditation bodies have understood the importance of communicating aims to learners and have set this requirement for teachers, but without effectively explaining their importance. They have only scratched the surface by explaining the 'what' and not the 'why' of aims.

Category 3 is perhaps the most problematic, as in this situation even the teacher is not aware of their aims and objectives. Very often when working with materials provided by institutions or with coursebooks the 'aim' of the lesson might be considered covering everything in the materials or getting from point A to point B in a specified period of time. Teachers in these situations focus on how much of the material has been covered as opposed to how much has been learnt.

The issue is that in all of these situations, teachers are relying on learners to:

- have good learning habits;
- interpret the stages of the lesson;
- understand the reason for these stages;
- know the aims of a coursebook or particular piece of material;
- and (most challenging of all!) judge their own attainment.

Where might Covert Teaching come from?

Discussing learning means listening to what our learners have to say, not only about *what* we have taught them but also *how* we taught it. This can feel quite exposing even for experienced teachers. For newly-qualified teachers in particular it can be an extremely daunting concept.

Learning to teach a language is full of challenges and obstacles which can stand in the way of Overt Teaching. For some teachers, their teaching journey begins with a short course, which may or may not include observed teaching practice. They are then handed a coursebook and sent into the classroom to teach a group of expectant learners who, depending on the context, may have different educational backgrounds, spiky profiles of language and skills knowledge, and a range of ages, interests, needs, goals and even levels.

David certainly experienced this. In his first teaching job, he was handed a coursebook and some CDs and sent to teach off-site in a building with no staffroom or colleagues. He had fifteen learners in one group, some of whom were upper intermediate (B2) level, some of whom were preparing for the Cambridge First Certificate exam, meaning they were interested in learning high-stakes exam skills, and some of whom were advanced (C1) level. He fell back on what he knew: covering the activities in the book. He didn't know why exactly each activity was important and he worried about being asked questions he couldn't answer, so he was defensive if learners asked why they were doing something.

Mark's first teaching job was a similar sink-or-swim introduction to teaching. While he was lucky enough to join a supportive staffroom with lots of energy and ideas, every term coursebooks would rotate and teachers would be assigned new classes and new levels, meaning he was constantly trying to get to grips with new material, focusing more on the items that needed to be covered and less on whether those items were being retained by learners or could be used in a meaningful context. High staff turnover meant that soon Mark was considered one of the more experienced teachers and was tasked with supporting new teachers.

In both situations, we were learning that teaching meant covering items in our materials. In Mark's situation, he was not only learning this but passing this lesson on to newer teachers as they joined the staffroom.

We hope that many readers had more positive beginnings, but we are sure others can empathise with the feeling of isolation and the high expectations placed on teachers by their learners, their institutions, national curriculums or even themselves. It is easy to understand why our coursebooks become our teaching buoy when we are awash in a sea of uncertainty. Covering easily ticked-off lexical and grammatical items which can be systematically prepared before the lesson gives new teachers some structure, a structure they are often reluctant to experiment with. It is important to note here that our issue as writers is not with coursebooks or grammar; instead, we are saying that it is completely understandable that newly-qualified teachers learn what makes a successful lesson from the material in front of them, and in general coursebooks and other published teaching materials do not contain activities in which teachers or learners are encouraged to discuss learning.

It might seem difficult to see how a teacher using their coursebook as a guide could become an Overt Teacher. Experience of teaching which is restricted to working within the confines of the coursebook will not necessarily lead to a more overt approach to teaching. As Penny Ur mentions in *A Course in Language Teaching* there are teachers with twenty years' experience and those with one year's experience repeated twenty times (1996, p317). That said, we do believe there is a confidence that comes with time and experience. It is often easier for an experienced teacher to acknowledge to a class that there is something they don't know. An experienced teacher might be happier to discuss it as a group or to explain that they will come back to their learners with an answer at a later date. For a new teacher, or even an experienced teacher who is working with a new group of learners, admitting to vulnerability can be a daunting prospect. There is a feeling that if we admit to not knowing something, we will expose our lack of experience and lose the faith of our learners.

Teachers having a Covert Approach to teaching is not really a surprise. The factors described above provide the perfect conditions for the creation of teachers who take the role of 'expert' in the classroom, but who are reluctant to take or answer questions about the aims of their lesson or activities. These are teachers who care about their learners' learning but who don't necessarily know how to discuss it with the learners themselves.

What research supports Overt Teaching?

Much has been written about evidence-based learning, visible learning and knowing your impact as a teacher. One of the key researchers in this area is John Hattie. With his various collaborators, he has written extensively since 2008, when he first published his book *Visible Learning*. On page 1 of his 2012 book, Hattie explains what this means:

> The "visible" aspect refers first to making students' learning visible to teachers, ensuring clear identification of the attributes that make a visible difference to student learning, and all in the school visibly knowing the impact that they have on the learning in the school (of the student, teacher, and school leaders). The 'visible' aspect also refers to making teaching visible to the student, such that they learn to become their own teachers, which is the core attribute of lifelong learning or self-regulation, and of the love of learning that we so want students to value. The 'learning' aspect refers to how we go about knowing and understanding, and then doing something about student learning.

In this book Hattie brought together 800 meta-analyses on what influences achievement and learning. A meta-analysis is a statistical procedure in which researchers bring together data from a number of independent studies of the same subject, with the aim of uncovering overall trends. The meta-analyses Hattie studied covered more than 80 million learners, examining the impact of every aspect of a school and classroom on learning. In this ongoing Visible Learning project, Hattie and his collaborators aim 'to move from "what works" [in teaching] to "what works best" and when, for whom, and why.' (Hattie and Zierer, 2018, p XVIII). The idea is that teachers and school managers have evidence of learners progressing or of their approach and efforts working, but much of that evidence is experiential and anecdotal. Hattie aimed to find actual evidence of the impact of every aspect of the school and classroom on learning, establishing what it was that had the biggest impact on learning. His aim was to move from the anecdotal to the visible.

From 2008 to 2018, Hattie and his collaborators added to the original meta-analyses, bringing the total from 800 to over 1400 meta-analyses, covering an estimated quarter of a million learners (Hattie and Zierer, 2018). The study covered learners from two to twenty years old, in various contexts around the world, studying everything from English to music. In terms of effect, one of the interesting things Hattie and his collaborators discovered was that subject matter did not have a large effect on achievement, meaning it was not necessarily important *what* you were studying, but rather *how* you were learning it.

Based on his research, Hattie published a ranked list of 138 influences on learning in his 2008 book *Visible Learning*. The list is constantly being updated on the Visible Learning blog at http://visible-learning.org. These factors cover a wide range of aspects that could have an effect on learning, from more teaching-focused ones like teacher clarity and teaching strategies, to institutional factors like class sizes and extra-curricular programmes. It even includes home-life factors such as family structure and parental involvement.

Hattie and his collaborators calculated an effect size for each factor so that the effect of each one on educational achievement was visible and their influence on learning could be more easily compared. Effect sizes are commonly used in statistics to establish how meaningful the relationship between different variables is and to allow you to compare these relationships between groups. Each factor in his study was given a score of 0 to 1, based on the effect it has on learning and progression across a year of study. According to Hattie and Zierer (2018), the scores can be interpreted as:

- Less than 0.0 is considered a negative effect on achievement.
- 0.1 to 0.2 is considered a low effect on achievement.
- 0.3 to 0.4 is considered a medium effect on achievement.
- Greater than 0.4 is considered a high effect on achievement.

It can be useful to group the various factors into categories to see where the largest effect lies. As can be seen in the table below (Hattie and Zierer, 2018, p XIX), the study found that the areas with the largest effects are 'Teacher', 'Teaching' and 'Curriculum'.

Factors	Overall Effect Size
Teacher	0.47
Curriculum	0.45
Teaching	0.43
Learners	0.39
Family	0.31
School	0.23

Teachers clearly have a substantial effect on their learners, with the potential to have a truly positive effect on learning. This does not mean we should ignore other factors such as Family, Learners or School, but some of these areas might be beyond our control. The question for teachers is therefore: where can we focus our efforts to have the greatest impact on our learners' achievement? To refer back to Hattie's quote earlier in this section, it can't just be about 'what works', it has to be about 'what works best'.

Feedback

In Hattie's original list of 138 factors, feedback was one of the top ten factors, with an effect size of 0.74, meaning it has one of the biggest effects on learning. In 2018, John Hattie and Klaus Zierer published their book *10 Mindframes for Visible Learning*. In this book, they viewed the same data from another angle, looking to establish the story behind the data. They provided ten teacher mindframes that led to visible learning. Their sixth mindframe was 'I give and help students understand feedback and I interpret and act on feedback given to me' (pV). Hattie and Zierer see feedback as a two-way street, explaining that 'teachers are thus capable both of giving learners feedback on their learning processes and of demanding and interpreting feedback from learners on their own teaching processes' (p75).

The idea that feedback involves both learners and teachers is at the heart of Overt Teaching, which emphasises the importance of the dialogic nature of effective feedback. This is what enables us to put our learners at the centre of their own learning discussion. How can we as teachers work with our learners to make decisions about how best to proceed without the benefit of free-flowing feedback: feedback from us to them, from them to us, and from peer to peer?

If we accept that feedback is central to making learning visible to learners, to involving our learners in the learning discussion, and therefore to Overt Teaching, then what are some of the potential barriers to effective feedback? If a teacher is acting covertly and 'hiding' the tools a learner needs to be able to give and interpret feedback, then feedback can appear in only one format: from teacher to learner, blocking other potentially useful forms of feedback. At the start of an activity, if a learner is unaware as to what exactly is expected of them from a skills and linguistic point of view, then their tendency will be to focus on task or content achievement. This is likely to lead to them sticking to 'safe' language and skills, the language and skills they arrived in the lesson with that day, rather than experimenting with something new. In this situation, what format will feedback inevitably take? It will not be feedback focused on what has been achieved in terms of language and skills development, and what the next steps are to achieve further; instead, it will most likely be content-based feedback or error correction focusing on a range of errors learners made while completing a task, errors that may or may not be relevant to the aims of the lesson. With truly effective, dialogic feedback being the goal, this book will focus on how the Overt Teacher creates the conditions for this feedback in their lessons.

Key principles of an Overt Teacher

Introduction

So, what is an Overt Teacher and what can they achieve? A teacher who is teaching overtly engages their learners in the discussion of learning and dialogic feedback around learning. They place their learners firmly at the centre of the learning discussion, as opposed to it only moving in a single direction from teacher to learner. While this might seem a worthy goal, it can be often be challenging to take that first step. We would suggest that it begins with a set of key principles.

Key principles of Overt Teaching

1. An Overt Teacher believes learners should know **what they are learning**.
2. An Overt Teacher believes learners should know **why they are learning it**, namely how the things they are learning can be applied to their lives outside the classroom.
3. An Overt Teacher believes that a learner should be **involved in discussions about what they are learning**.
4. An Overt Teacher believes learners will benefit from **choosing and discussing their own levels of success**.
5. An Overt Teacher believes that learners should be involved in **dialogic feedback about their success**.

Throughout this book we will examine various strategies to help you build on these principles and bring your learners to the centre of their learning. Much like the toolbox of teaching activities or language practice tasks that you can already draw from when the need arises, by the end of this book you will have a toolbox of techniques for discussing learning with your learners and enabling dialogic feedback. We will now consider each of these principles in turn, grouping them where appropriate.

Key principles 1, 2 and 3: Aims and objectives – beginning discussions so learners know what they are learning and why

Our first three principles can be grouped together as each informs the other. The idea is that learners should know what they are learning and why, considering how will it help them in their lives outside the classroom. It is not enough to tell learners this information, they must be involved in this discussion throughout the lesson. Learners are the key stakeholders in any lesson and each of them brings their own learning needs to the classroom. It is through discussion around these needs that our learners can personalise the content of the lesson and apply it to their own lives. Effective and accessible aims and objectives provide the scaffolding and support for these discussions.

What are aims and objectives?

It is important to begin with our definitions of both terms, as there have been many interpretations over the years. As Thornbury (2011) argues, 'the concept of aims seems to be based on the fallacy that language learning is the incremental accumulation of discrete items of linguistic knowledge'. This idea that aims are just items to be ticked off on a long list of lexical or grammatical items is not how we see them. When discussing lesson planning, Scrivener describes procedural aims, 'what students will do during class', and achievement aims, 'what the teacher hopes the students will achieve by doing them' (2011, p136). When exploring their mindframe, 'I explicitly inform students what successful impact looks like from the outset' (2018, p117), Hattie and Zierer use the term 'learning objectives', explaining that they 'reveal what the goal of learning is' (2018, p122). Throughout his various books on visible learning, Hattie and his collaborators also refer to 'learning intentions' where the focus is placed more on expected learning as opposed to projected learning.

For the purposes of this book we define an aim and an objective as follows:

- **Objective:** this is the final goal of the lesson. This is what the learners will be better able to do by the end of the lesson.
- **Aim:** this is a key learning stage in the lesson, one of the steps the learners will take in order to achieve the objective.

Writing real-life objectives

The learning journey begins with knowing where you want to end up. Once the destination has been decided, we can make decisions about the best way to get there. Hattie argues that 'effective teachers plan effectively by deciding on appropriately challenging goals and then structuring situations so that learners can reach these goals' (2012, p47). On her website, Shirley Clarke reminds us that 'All learners need to know learning objectives in order to have a chance of succeeding.' In English teaching, this begins with a real-life objective that we can move towards with our learners.

Let's start with an example. Imagine that you are learning English as a second language. You are an intermediate (B1) learner and you have been studying in your current school for 20 weeks. You walk into your lesson and see these aims displayed on the board.

Aims:

- Present perfect
- Past simple
- Should
- Activities vocabulary

Questions begin to form in your mind:

- What will I actually be able to do after this lesson?
- How is this relevant to my life outside the classroom?
- Why am I seeing the present perfect again?

It is questions like these that can lead to early disengagement from learners, and even cries of 'But we've already done that, teacher!' The problem is that this is a list of items that will be covered in the lesson rather than clear learning or teaching aims.

Reflection

- What effect might these aims have on the learner?
- What real-life objective could you add to these aims?

Read on to check your ideas.

In the above example, there is no real thread linking one item to the next for the learner and therefore no clear goal. The learner is aware they are learning grammar and vocabulary but not how it might benefit them outside the lesson. Seeing the present perfect as an aim, and one that (depending on their level) they have likely encountered before, could cause some disengagement and even frustration. If the learner were to ask themselves 'What will I be better able to do at the end of this lesson?' the only reasonable answer would be 'I will be better able to complete exercises on the present perfect and past simple', which is probably not what the teacher intended. Completing exercises might be a means to an end, but in a communicative language classroom, it should not really be the end in itself.

Adding a statement beginning 'By the end of the lesson, you will be (better) able to…' provides the learners with an objective, making it clear what direction the lesson is heading in. For example:

Aims:
- Present perfect
- Past simple
- Should
- Activities vocabulary

Objective:
By the end of the lesson, you will be better able to ask for and give recommendations in a new city.

Beginning the dialogue with an objective

It is now clear what learners will be able to do at the end of the lesson, meaning the focus has moved away from the aims and onto the objective. In her paper 'Communicating Learning Goals and Success Criteria with Students', Nancy Gerzon writes that communication of learning goals does not just mean 'that teachers post the goal on the classroom whiteboard, but that learners have a clear understanding of what the goal and the Success Criteria entail.' Success criteria are a list of criteria for the success of a particular task, which helps learners to plan, visualise and assess success. We will address success criteria in more detail in **Part A, Key principle 4: Choosing and discussing success**.

In the same paper, Gerzon argues that learners' understanding of the learning goal, or objective, for a lesson cannot be achieved or assessed without discussion. One-way communication is not sufficient. Robin Alexander and Frank Hardman led the Dialogic Teaching research project, which ran across primary schools in England between 2014 and 2017. Over the course of this project, participating teachers found that after moving to a more questioning, dialogic approach in their lessons, there were 'direct positive gains from the programme for classroom talk, pupil engagement and pupil learning' (2017, p6). While this study was not carried out in English language classrooms, the results are still interesting for us. They clearly showed an increase in engagement and attainment when learners were encouraged to question and discuss the content and learning of the lesson. In Overt Teaching this dialogue begins with the objective of the lesson.

Reflection
What questions could you ask intermediate (B1) learners to begin a dialogue about this objective?

Objective
By the end of the lesson, you will be better able to ask for and give recommendations in a new city.

Read on to check your ideas.

There are many questions you could ask but the key is to encourage learners to engage with the objective, considering not just why it is important within the confines of the classroom but also in their lives. For the example above, some possible questions would be:

1. Can you give recommendations for things to do in a city? What language would you use?
2. How do you think what we are learning today will help you to give recommendations in a city?
3. When will you be able to use these recommendations in your real life?
4. In what other situations might you ask for or give recommendations?

Questions 1 and 2 encourage learners to reflect on where they currently are: what knowledge they are bringing to the lesson and what they still need to learn. Together the teacher and learner can begin to uncover learners' individual needs. If a learner gets frustrated and says, 'But teacher, I can do this already', the teacher can begin to deal with it by eliciting how well the learner can actually ask for or give recommendations and highlighting the gaps in their knowledge which this lesson will fill. Without this initial dialogue, it is probable that the teacher will remain uninformed, and the learner will remain frustrated.

When discussing engagement and bridging the gap between the curricular and extracurricular spheres, Mercer and Dörnyei (2020, p15) note that it can 'be a real challenge to create a connection between the two spheres. However, if it can be done, for the majority of learners, this will be a considerable boost that helps them to see the real-world relevance of the language and to make its use personally relevant.' We couldn't agree with them more and feel that while it is indeed challenging to do this, it is worthwhile and can make a huge difference to learner engagement. This is what Questions 3 and 4 aim to do. After all, how can we expect learners to link lesson content to the real world if we do not give them the space within the lesson to do so? We also cannot assume that all learners will apply the objective to their lives in the same way. The discussion that emerges from these guiding questions allows the learners, with the support of their teacher, to consider how best it applies to their contexts.

Objective discussion in practice

Let's have a look at how this kind of discussion might work in a classroom. Here is a summary of a conversation David observed in a lesson which had the same objective as we discussed in the previous section:

Learner A: OK, question 2. When will you be able to practise this conversation in your real life?

Learner B: I don't know. I don't have a holiday this year.

Learner A: Ah, OK. Difficult.

Teacher: Well, do you have anything new this year?

Learner B: I will go to university.

Learner A: And I will have a new job…I hope.

Teacher: Do you think you could use this language to ask for or give recommendations in these situations? How would that work?

In the conversation the learners have the chance to discuss why they might not feel the lesson is appropriate for their context. Hattie and Clarke speak about communicating the 'big picture', helping learners to see how the various pieces of the lesson fit together in advance, 'a secret we have often not let students into'. Without this opportunity to understand the big picture, this feeling of not knowing a lesson's relevance is one that will most likely remain unspoken and could lead to demotivation.

In the conversation above, the teacher communicates the big picture but goes further by engaging the learners in a dialogue. Their worries are addressed and they can see how the lesson is relevant to them. Although the learners haven't chosen the content, they have been given the chance to understand how to personalise it for their specific contexts. They can see what they are learning and why it is useful for them. From the first few minutes of the lesson, they have already begun to bridge the gap between what they will learn and their lives.

Another way of helping learners to see beyond the lesson is to ensure your objectives are real-life but without naming a specific context. Hattie and Clarke give the example of the difference between 'learning to design a poster for a holiday in St Lucia' and 'learning to design a poster' (Hattie and Clarke, 2019, p54). The latter is a decontextualised, transferrable skill which they say 'is transferable to different contexts', while the former is more specific and would rely on discussion between the learner and teacher to uncover that transferability. Taking the objective from the example lesson above, we could rewrite it as 'By the end of the lesson, you will be better able to ask for and give recommendations (e.g. in a new city).' While the initial objective was a transferrable skill, by highlighting that *in a new city* is an example of where this language and skill can be used, the transferability of the objective can be made more transparent to learners.

Knowing your why: Moving from coursebooks to objectives

Many teachers are required to use coursebooks or institutionally created materials as the basis for their lessons. This can lead to an impression that grammar points or sets of vocabulary are the aim of lessons. The following steps can help teachers to uncover the reasons behind these language points so they can better discuss them with their learners.

▸ Step 1: Why now?

It can be a good idea to examine why this language point is being focused on at this particular stage in the course. Consider the present perfect simple arising as a point to be addressed mid-way through an Intermediate (B1) course. Is it being introduced as a language point for the first time? Are learners encountering a new use of it? Is it being revised so that it can be used as part of a communicative task? This knowledge can inform the approach a teacher will take in their lesson.

▸ Step 2: How is it being used?

The next step would be to examine function. Keeping with the example of present perfect simple, teachers can explore what function of the language point is being presented. Is it about recently finished actions, asking about experiences or something else? Have their learners encountered previous functions that this is adding to?

▸ Step 3: How can learners use it outside the classroom?

Now that the teacher knows why this point is being introduced and what function is being addressed, they are better prepared to discuss with their learners how this language point applies to their life, why it is relevant for them to learn it.

Taking this approach means teachers are better placed to decide what their learners need from a lesson; including what to omit from the coursebook, how long to spend on each section, or which extra materials might be needed.

While the example above is grammar related, this approach can also be used for skills activities. Whether it is a reading, speaking, listening or writing skill asking the questions above can help guide teachers in how to approach this skill in their lesson. Is it only being practised and therefore their learners' attention merely needs to be drawn to the skill? Or, is this a new skill they have not encountered before, requiring overt discussion on how best to approach this activity?

As a teacher, taking the time to consider why you are doing particular activities, language points and skills activities from your materials can make it easier to justify your choices to the learners and give your lessons a sharper focus. You will be:

- better placed to deliver more effective lessons for learners, with clearer learning objectives;
- better able to respond to learners' questions about why you are focusing on a particular area;
- better able to negotiate learning needs with your learners.

'Knowing the why' can also help with lesson planning, the wording of your aims, and ultimately the writing and production of more effective materials.

Discussing objectives

In our experience, discussing objectives works best as short conversations that are conducted frequently throughout a lesson, for example as part of task instructions or feedback stages, as reminders of the lesson objectives. As well as making the classroom less teacher-centric, we can discover what our learners understand about our objectives and assess how well we ourselves understand them.

To ensure they are real conversations, rather than one-sided monologues, learners need to come to these discussions as active partners in their learning, rather than the more passive role they have in the traditional learner-teacher model which they may have previously experienced, where the teacher makes all content decisions. Depending on what learners have experienced before, they may be reluctant to take part in these discussions at first, as it requires them to take a more active part in their own learning. However, we have found that with time and support, this initial reluctance is replaced with enthusiasm from learners who feel more autonomous and able to take an active role in their learning.

Effective aims

Having a real-life objective allows learners to see where they are going. Effective aims help them to see exactly how they will get there. In the example we discussed previously about recommendations, the aims are quite broad, and the learner has to do a lot of work to understand how they relate to the objective.

Reflection

Read the two versions of the aims in the box below.
Why do you think the second version might be more useful to learners?
Read on to check your ideas.

Version 1

Aims:

- Present perfect
- Past simple
- Should
- Activities vocabulary

Objective:
By the end of the lesson, you will be better able to ask for and give recommendations in a new city.

Version 2

Aims:

- To learn to ask about experience using the present perfect.
- To revise talking about a past experience using the past simple.
- To practise giving advice using 'should'.
- To learn to talk about common activities in a city using longer lexical chunks.

Objective:
By the end of the lesson, you will be better able to ask for and give recommendations in a new city.

To be effective, an aim must clearly build towards the objective and contain clear guidance on how it will be achieved, helping the learner to see the steps towards reaching the objective. Learners should not be left to guess the relevance of the major aims of the lesson, as they need to in Version 1. It should be clear from the start of the lesson.

In Version 2, most aims contain three parts. Each part serves a clear purpose in informing the learner: study verbs, function, and language point / skill / range of lexis. In the table below we examine them in more detail.

Part	Study verb	Function	Language point / Skill / Range of lexis
Examples	To learn To revise To practise	to ask about experience talking about a past experience giving advice to talk about common activities in a city	the present perfect the past simple 'should' using longer lexical chunks
Comment	Choosing the appropriate study verb, gives the learner clear guidance on how this aim will be achieved. It informs learners whether this is new information, or a new use of old information, managing expectations from the beginning of the lesson.	The function focuses the learners' attention on the exact use of the language point, skill or items of lexis. Placing it before the language point prioritises the function over the language itself and keeps the focus of the lesson on the communicative outcome as opposed to covering items of language.	Here, learners can see what language points will be learnt or how their prior knowledge will be applied to a different function.

Formatting aims and objectives consistently

There are many possible stumbling blocks on the road to the effective discussion of learning in a lesson. It is important that as many of these obstacles as possible are removed, allowing both learners and teachers to focus on the discussion itself.

One obstacle could be the language used in the aims. If it is above the level of the learners or contains too much metalanguage (technical terminology used to describe language and learning), learners will waste valuable time trying to understand the language instead of focusing on the discussion itself. Of course, if an understanding of some metalanguage will help learners to hold discussions of aims and objectives, then perhaps spending some lesson time on teaching it could be beneficial.

Another stumbling block is inconsistency. If the format or manner in which aims and objectives are communicated changes from lesson to lesson, learners will have to spend lesson time trying to understand them instead of discussing them. However you choose to communicate them, in our experience consistency is crucial: consistency of language level, language type and format. This will ensure your learners can quickly and easily identify what they will be learning that day and you can immediately engage them in a discussion without learners having to orientate themselves afresh each time. If learners have to work to identify the objective or if teachers have to spend time explaining metalanguage, valuable time is being wasted, time which could be spent on the discussion of learning.

While you may have some institutional requirements for how and when your objectives are communicated, here are four possible formats for communicating aims and objectives to learners:

Option 1: Infinitives and 'By the end of the lesson...'

Aims:
- To learn to ask about experience using the present perfect.
- To revise talking about a past experience using the past simple.
- To practise giving advise using "should".
- To learn vocabulary for common activities in a city.

Objective:
By the end of the lesson, you will be better able to ask for and give recommendations (e.g. in a new city).

Option 2: 'In this lesson, we will...'

In this lesson, we will:
- Learn to ask about experience using the present perfect.
- Revise talking about a past experience using the past simple.
- Practise giving advice using *should*.
- Learn vocabulary for common activities in a city.

So that you are better able to:
Ask for and give recommendations (e.g. in a new city).

Option 3: The Story

Today we're going to learn to ask for and give recommendations in a new city. First of all, we're going to brainstorm and learn vocabulary for common activities you might do in a city. Then, we'll learn to ask about experience using the present perfect. Then we'll revise talking about past experience using the past simple. And finally, we'll practise giving advice, using *should* and the activities vocabulary. At the end of the lesson, you're going to imagine your partner is visiting your city, they're going to ask for recommendations and you're going to give them. Then we'll get feedback, swap over and try again.

Option 4: We are learning to... / What I'm looking for...

We are learning to (WALT):
- Ask for and give recommendations in a new city.

What I'm looking for (WILF):
- Asking about experience using the present perfect.
- Talking about a past experience using the past simple.
- Giving advice using 'should'.
- A range of vocabulary for common activities in a city.

Reflection
Which of these formats do you think would be most applicable to your context or beneficial to your learners? Read on for our analysis.

Analysis of different formats

Options 1 and 2 are noticeably similar to each other. Personally, we prefer the latter as there is no need to establish the difference in meaning between an aim and an objective, something that we have dedicated an entire portion of this book to, and which is therefore perhaps not something we should require of our learners. David first saw Option 2 used on a teacher's board during an observation. It was immediately clear to everyone what they were doing and why because of the slightly narrative nature of the wording.

Option 3 expands on this idea of narrative. It is perhaps more challenging for learners to identify the various aims, but one colour of text can be used to identify the objective and another colour to identify the key aims. This approach can help to scaffold their understanding but once again consistency is key. If the colour is changed regularly, it can be confusing for learners. The benefit of this approach is that it allows the teacher to easily discuss how each section links to the next and to include some of the key stages of the lesson that build towards achievement of the final objective but are not necessarily a learning aim (e.g. 'Then we'll get feedback', 'Swap over and try again').

Option 4 is often attributed to Shirley Clarke and is slightly different to the other options as instead of focusing on the learning aims, 'What I'm looking for... (WILF)' presents the success criteria and 'We are learning to... (WALT)' is the learning objective. You may wish to avoid using WILF / WALT as acronyms, as this could requiring extra processing from students. As Hattie and Zierer (2018, p121) explain, 'learning objectives and success criteria are two sides of a coin and are mutually dependent on each other regarding their effect.' We would argue that a discussion in which success criteria are created based on the aims is a valuable part of the learning process and should not be missed. We will look at success criteria in more detail in ⏩ **Part A, Key principle 4: Choosing and discussing success**.

Dialogue in action

Now let's visit an English for Work class which Mark once observed. The group of learners were from very different backgrounds, levels and workplaces. The teacher was focussing on email conventions in the workplace. She discussed the learners' own working needs at the beginning of the lesson. As the lesson progressed, she would refer back to this discussion, highlighting to one learner when a task was particularly important for them or to another when it might not be crucial for them to be able to produce the language in their context but that it would be useful to understand. There was an honesty and dialogue to her lesson which the learners clearly appreciated. They knew when they needed to take particular notice and when they didn't. Each learner was working towards the objective of 'writing effective emails' in their own way, with a focus on their own context. This dialogue was possible because the teacher had clearly displayed and discussed her aims and objective at the beginning of the lesson. This discussion had set the tone for the whole lesson.

The teacher had effective aims and a real-life objective with a consistent format, and her learners could see where they were going and how they were going to get there. In traditional lessons, aims are often seen as a one-way street, something that learners are informed of and have to accept. However, all learners come to the lesson with different strengths, weaknesses, knowledge gaps, needs and desires. It would be unrealistic to assume they all need exactly the same level of input in all areas, and this is what the English for Work teacher recognised. We can also assume that learners have an idea of their own strengths and weaknesses. Bringing this out in the open and discussing it with learners can help them to identify which sections of the lesson would be most important to them, and helps the teacher to signpost these sections of the lesson as it progresses.

Having said that, it is important to remember that when discussing aims and objectives teachers might not always receive the answer they are looking for. The desire is that all learners announce that the teacher's proposed aims are very relevant and useful to their context and they are immediately engaged in the lesson. However, this will not always be the case; teachers might not get the answers they want, but they will get the answers they need. For example, imagine a lesson in which one of the aims is 'checking someone's experience using present perfect questions'. As part of the dialogue about the aim, it emerges that a number of learners covered the present perfect in a grammar class yesterday and feel they do not need to look at it again. Understandably the teacher might be frustrated about their carefully planned lesson, but actually they can now make informed decisions about how long to spend on that section of the lesson. They can also explain to learners that they will not be introducing the present perfect again but rather giving them the opportunity to practise what they learnt yesterday in a different context.

Hattie and Zierer (2018, p123) summarise this idea:

> Visibility of learning objectives and addressing the success criteria lead to the fact that the learners can better understand where they are in the learning process, where they have their strengths and weaknesses, and where the dissonance between the can-do and the cannot-yet-do lies.

Without making the learning objectives visible, it will be challenging, or perhaps even impossible, for some learners and teachers to have the discussions they need to in order to ensure that learning will be as efficient and useful as possible.

Another example of informed teaching through dialogue might be opening up the discussion of pronunciation and context. Consider a lesson that involves teaching connected speech, the way in which sounds can be merged together, altered or omitted in fast speech. While this might be beneficial for many in the class, perhaps a number of the learners work in international companies where English is the main medium for communication but it tends not to be the first language of the employees. In this situation using connected speech might actually make them less comprehensible. However, it might be beneficial for the learners to be able to recognise weak forms in speech if they regularly meet with clients from English-speaking countries. Whatever their context, this discussion would help the teacher to frame the pronunciation section of the lesson so that it meets the needs of the whole class instead of just some learners.

Once informed, the teacher can make decisions throughout the lesson and refer back to what was discussed at the beginning. In this way, the teacher can ensure that while the learning aims and objectives were chosen by them (or maybe dictated by curriculum needs), the lesson itself is personalised to the needs and interests of the individual learners with the discussion continuing throughout the lesson, as in the classroom we visited at the start of this section.

Outcome mining

One criticism that may be levelled at learning aims is that they are rigid constraints decided before the lesson which cannot be changed, adapted or built on during the lesson. However, the idea is not that teachers dictate objectives to learners, but that they engage learners in a dialogue around these objectives throughout the lesson.

Because conversations take place from the outset of the lesson, the teacher and the learners are informed, meaning that as new language and skills needs arise throughout the lesson, they can make decisions on how best to manage this language. In this example, the aims and objective are:

Today we are going to:
- Learn about some common Canadian food and drink
- Learn to describe the cooking process (using cooking verbs)
- Learn to organise a process so it is easy for a listener to follow (using linking words)

So that you can:
- Tell someone how a dish is made (e.g. Canadian dishes)

Imagine that in the lesson, learners began to react both positively and negatively to the food that was being described and the teacher ended up teaching the lexical chunks below:
- 'That sounds (delicious / disgusting / interesting).'
- 'I'm not really a fan of ________ food.'
- 'I'm not sure that's for me.'

This language had not been planned by the teacher, but it will help learners achieve their objective more naturally if they can tell someone how a dish is made and reply appropriately. This language can be incorporated easily into the final task and emerged from learners' needs during the lesson.

We will refer to this unintended (but relevant) learning that can emerge throughout a lesson, rather than being planned before the lesson, as outcomes. Outcomes, if they contribute to the objective, are no less valid than pre-planned lesson aims. With this in mind, it is often a good idea to carry out some outcome mining, meaning that the teacher and learners spend some time at the end of the lesson reflecting on the unintended learning opportunities that arose during the lesson, and the language and skills that emerged over the course of the lesson. To find out more, see **Part B, Chapter 4, 'Post-lesson outcome mining'**.

Key principle 4: Choosing and discussing success

Key principle 4 is that learners benefit from choosing and discussing their own levels of success. Knowing what they are studying and why is crucial, but it is equally important to know what success looks like, and therefore be able to reflect on and discuss their own levels of success. As Hattie and Clarke (2019, p58) say,

> Once the learner has success criteria they have a framework for a formative dialogue, with peers or adults.

Imagine a lesson in which the objective is 'By the end of the lesson, learners will be better able to discuss their plans.' The teacher has taught various language chunks for common activities, they have taught 'be going to' for plans and present continuous to talk about fixed arrangements, and they have taught various language chunks for commenting on people's plans (e.g. 'oh lovely' / 'sounds like fun'). All of this builds towards the final communicative task of discussing plans for the weekend. It is time for the final task and the teacher gives their instructions, which they check carefully: learners are to stand up, find someone they haven't spoken to yet that lesson and tell each other their plans; when the teacher claps their hands, the learners are to move and find a new partner and repeat the activity. Everything is ready to go. The learners find their partners, the teacher signals for them to begin, the learners start talking and for the most part they all fall back on their 'safe language', the language they arrived at the lesson with. Most of the learners are using 'will' to discuss all of their plans, very few of the language chunks from the lesson are attempted and the learners are not commenting on each other's plans.

Reflection
- Why do you think this might have happened?
- What could the teacher have done differently in this situation?

Read on to check your ideas.

In this situation, the teacher has set up the task but has not taken the time to discuss what they expect success in that task to look like. Their instructions have communicated that success is achieved by:
- ☐ Finding a learner you have not spoken to.
- ☐ Telling them your plans.
- ☐ Moving to a new learner when the teacher claps.
- ☐ Telling the new learner about your plans.

The criteria are clear enough that the learners would no doubt be successful if they had had their attention drawn to them. The effective use of success criteria can ensure that both the teacher and learners have the same idea of success prior to the task. Once this has been achieved, the conditions are set for learners to attempt success and have discussions regarding this success with both their teacher and their peers.

What exactly are success criteria?

Success criteria clearly outline the factors that would indicate success in a given task. Imagine a lesson in which the teacher wants their English for Work class to be better able to give an elevator pitch, a brief presentation that usually introduces the speaker and a single idea or proposal. Elevator pitches are often used in business and are so named because it should take the same amount of time as you would expect to ride in an elevator with someone for. Learners might demonstrate success in the final task by 'giving an engaging, informative elevator pitch'. However, words like engaging and informative can be quite subjective and difficult to quantify. They can be understood differently depending on who the listener is and what they bring to the conversation. Clearer, more specific criteria help learners to more easily visualise what success would look like. Depending on the level of the group, the success criteria for an elevator pitch could look something like this:

Successfully giving an engaging, informative elevator pitch means:

- ☐ Delivering your pitch in no more than 2 minutes.
- ☐ Keeping your audience's attention throughout by:
  - ☐ Maintaining eye-contact with each person in turn.
  - ☐ Emphasising key words by stressing them.
  - ☐ Using your body language to emphasise these key words.
- ☐ Following the elevator pitch structure (highlight a problem > give a solution > get agreement > seal the deal).
- ☐ Use 'Have you ever…' to highlight a problem.
- ☐ Use 'What if I told you… / would you…?' to give a solution and get agreement.
- ☐ Use language chunks from the lesson to seal the deal.

In the above example, we can see that there are different types of criteria.

- **Task criteria**
  These criteria set the parameters for the task and will be quite fixed. They could be related to the number of people that need to be spoken to or the number of words that need to be written. In the above example, a maximum time limit of two minutes is set.

- **Closed criteria**
  These criteria must be achieved and there is little to no element of choice. An example in the above criteria would be 'Following the elevator pitch structure'. This is a specific structure that has been given for this task and must be followed to achieve success.

- **Open criteria**
  An example from above would be 'Keeping your audience's attention throughout by…' and the list of possible options that follow. Learners are not expected to attempt all three of these sub-criteria, at least not in the first attempt, though they may work towards this with repeated attempts at the task. There is an element of choice in these open criteria, with everyone in the class working towards success but choosing their own way of achieving it. Hattie and Clarke (2019, p57) describe open criteria as 'difficult to quantify' and 'with a menu of possible items to include; optional rather than compulsory'. These open criteria will often be optional sub-criteria focusing on specific skills or language points that would help the learner to achieve this criterion. They can also be used for differentiation.

As we write this book, success criteria are not generally featured in coursebooks for English language teaching. One exception is the 2022 coursebook series *Voices* from National Geographic Learning, which includes success criteria for all writing tasks, though not for other task types. In exam teaching for IELTS, TOEFL or the Cambridge suite of exams, assessment criteria are often clearly laid out and become the criteria for success, but this is less true of general English materials. This is something we predict will change in the coming years with success criteria being given the importance of space on the page in coursebooks or at least being suggested in teacher's books. However, it is not just the presence of success criteria in materials that makes them effective, but rather the discussions around them which make them truly useful to learners.

There is more information about how to create success criteria in ⏩ **Part B, Chapter 3**.

Discussing success

When it comes to communicating what success in a given task looks like, there are two schools of thought. Success criteria can be communicated at the beginning of the lesson at the same time as the lesson objective so that learners can see from the outset what is expected of them. Alternatively, they can be communicated later in the lesson, providing learners with a challenge as they must discover the criteria throughout the lesson. Hattie and Zierer (2018, p119) highlight that the latter is more appropriate for lessons in which 'problem solving itself is the focus'. They suggest that the choice of approach very much 'depends on the goal of the lesson'.

Our personal feeling is that discussing aims and objectives is the first communication of what success looks like. The objective signals clearly what task will be achieved by the end of the lesson and the aims break down the various aspects that will make up success in this task.

This means that while specific success criteria will only be introduced and discussed just before the final communicative task, success itself is an ongoing conversation throughout the lesson. Success criteria themselves can then become a pre-task consolidation and planning tool, and a post-task tool for reflection and feedback. They can also incorporate language or skills points which have emerged during the lesson, which can be highlighted through outcome mining.

Co-constructing success criteria

At first glance, it may seem that simply presenting learners with the criteria for success and then letting them begin the task would be the quickest and easiest approach to communicating success. In one of his first attempts at using success criteria this was exactly what David did. It was a lesson on giving a spoken review of a film. After providing input, David presented learners with these criteria and set up the task:

A successful spoken review of a film:

- ☐ Follows the structure (introduction > story > recommendation).
- ☐ Uses present perfect questions to check if the listener has seen the film.
- ☐ Uses present simple to tell the story.
- ☐ Uses modal verbs to give a recommendation.
- ☐ Uses a range of film vocabulary from the lesson.

What he found, much to his frustration, was that learners largely ignored the criteria or applied them incorrectly, with one learner using the present simple to check if the listener had seen the film. On reflection and after further research into the topic, David realised he had not involved the learners in the creation of the criteria, nor had he given them the chance to see how they applied to a good or bad model of the task prior to the learners attempting the task for themselves.

Co-creating success criteria means involving your learners in the discussion of what success looks like. As Hattie and Clarke (2019, p66) say,

> ...being given a list of criteria without seeing them applied removes a crucial element of success – being able to see and analyse what a good one or different versions of good ones look like in advance.

This analysis can lead to a heightened awareness of what success looks like and therefore a greater level of learner independence when it comes to self-assessment and the assessment of others. This is a further reason to carry out the discussion of success prior to the final activity as opposed to at the outset of the lesson. To learn about how to use aims and objectives or models to co-create success criteria with learners, go to **Part B, Chapter 3**.

Varied success: managing differentiation in the classroom

Another advantage of success criteria is that they allow for differentiation in a class. Success does not have to be defined in the same way for every learner in the class. As we have already seen, there can be open criteria which involve a level of choice so all learners can move towards the same objective while demonstrating success in different ways. Even in a group with similar levels, no two learners will have exactly the same strengths and weaknesses. Depending on the teaching context, some learners may have been studying for longer than others or learners may be grouped by age as opposed to level. These are the realities of the English language classroom. Success criteria help the teacher to manage this differentiation, turning it into a positive learning discussion.

Depending on the task, there will probably be multiple indicators of success, some open and some closed. Attempting to achieve all of these in a single speaking task could be overwhelming for a learner if they feel each of them is slightly out of their comfort zone. This will most likely lead to the learners avoiding all or most of the criteria altogether or feeling frustrated by the task. To reduce the pressure, learners can discuss the success criteria before the task and choose which two or three they will personally focus on, saying how they will achieve the more open criteria. This element of choice opens up differentiation as a discussion in the lesson. As Hattie and Zierer (2018, p123) say, this helps each individual learner to find 'where the dissonance between the can-do and the cannot-yet-do lies' and informs the teacher of learners' intentions prior to the activity. This in turn sets the stage for personalised feedback that is meaningful for each learner, as opposed to generalised feedback relevant to only some learners. After all, if not everyone has attempted one aspect of a task, should they receive feedback on it? Probably not.

Let's take an example from a class Mark observed. It was a mixed level beginner and elementary class, studying with elementary (A2) materials. In this group there were also a number of learners in the group who were closer to pre-intermediate (A2/B1) and were soon going to take a level test. These were the aims and objectives that were communicated and discussed at the beginning of the lesson:

Today we are going to:

- Learn collocations for free time activities.
- Revise talking about activities we do (using free time).
- Read about people's free times and learn to talk about how often we do activities (using adverbs of frequency).
- Learn to show interest when someone is speaking.

So that you can:

- Talk about what you do in your free time.

Before the final task, the teacher played an example of a successful conversation and co-created these success criteria with their group:

When you talk about your free time, you should:

- ☐ Use 2-5 activity words from our lesson.
- ☐ Use the present simple to talk about activities you do.
- ☐ Use adverbs of frequency to talk about how often you do those activities.
- ☐ Show you are interested when people talk (using 'That sounds fun / interesting / nice.')

In this situation, expecting the beginner learners to meet, or even attempt, all of these success criteria the first time they try the task, would not only be unrealistic but probably overwhelming. Even for the elementary learners, knowing that adverbs of frequency and some of the collocations are probably new to them, expecting them to show interest as a listener as well might be too challenging for them. However, for those on their way to pre-intermediate (A2/B1), the final criterion might be just the challenge they need to ensure they feel they benefit from this activity. Allowing learners to choose which criteria they will focus on allows them to achieve success at their level to the best of their ability. Once learners are used to this process, they will be able to choose quite quickly, though it may take time and support for them to feel confident doing this.

For tips on managing these discussions, see **Part B, Chapter 3, 'Choosing success' and 'Visualising success'**.

Comfort zones

One possible criticism when it comes to learners choosing their own level of success is the belief that learners will choose 'safe' success, meaning they will only focus on criteria they can comfortably achieve and will not push themselves.

Some of this comes back to the choice of success, and the aims and objectives for a lesson. If those are too far removed from the ability of the learners, then it can 'invoke panic' in the learner (Hattie, and Clarke, 2019, p15). The aim is to plan a lesson with an appropriate level of challenge for the learners so that they find themselves slightly outside of their comfort zone. Inspired by the fairy tale, Hattie and Clarke refer to the 'Goldilocks principle' (ibid) of not too hard, not too easy, but just right. Hattie and Clarke add to this arguing that they must also not be too 'boring'. This is an interesting addition, the idea being that learners will often take on challenging tasks if they find them engaging (ibid). This idea of choice has led to creative approaches to discussing challenge like the 'Chilli Challenge' seen on Michael Plews' Big Blog of Teaching Ideas in which criteria are labelled 'mild', 'warm', 'spicy', or 'hot hot hot'. This kind of labelling can help learners to decide where their comfort zone is and what level of challenge they want to strive for. There are two important considerations when it comes to this kind of labelling, however. The first is the importance of remembering that learners are people and depending on what is going on in their lives outside the classroom, their choice of challenge may vary from one lesson to the next. The other is that by the teacher labelling criteria, they are imposing their view of challenge on learners, but the learners might not agree with the teacher on what is more or less challenging for them.

It is also important to remember that over the course of a lesson, something that may originally have been a challenge for a learner might stop being one as they learn and practise this area, especially if it is a known language point being applied in a new way. For example, the objective of a pre-intermediate (A2/B1) lesson is 'By the end of the lesson, learners will be better able to discuss their plans for the weekend'. This lesson might introduce the present continuous for fixed arrangements. While this might be a new application of the present continuous, we can assume learners at this level would already be aware of the form of present continuous and be able to produce it fairly accurately. This leaves them with only the single hurdle of applying it in a new context, something they may become more confident with throughout the lesson. The dialogue around comfort zones can therefore continue throughout the lesson, with learners having the option to change how they feel about a particular aim as new information arises

Success with reading and listening

In English language teaching, lessons in general English resource books and coursebooks tend to build towards a written or spoken communicative task. For this reason, the examples of lessons we've given so far have focused on these two areas. It is important to remember though that aims, objectives and success criteria can be outlined and discussed for receptive skills tasks as much as for productive skills. A useful approach when developing or practising skills to break them down into individual sub-skills. A sub-skill is a single skill that is part of a more complex skill. Writing, for example, would be the larger complex skill but in order to write an effective discursive essay, a learner would need to develop a range of sub-skills. Some examples of these could be:

- Essay organisation (i.e. paragraphing).
- Writing topic sentences.
- Supporting topic sentences with reasons and examples.
- Summarising and concluding information.
- Using linking phrases to ensure readers can follow your argument.

Let's take a reading skills lesson as an example. This lesson focuses on the sub-skill of reading a longer article quickly, often referred to as skim reading. The aims and objectives for the lesson are:

Today we will:
- Learn to predict the topic of a text.
- Learn strategies for skim-reading an article.
- Practise skim-reading online articles.

So that you can:
- Read a longer article quickly (e.g. to check whether you want to read it in more detail).

Reflection
What do you think the success criteria could be for this lesson?
Read on to check your ideas.

To help our learners to be able to assess and discuss their success, the teacher and learners will need to co-construct success criteria based on the practical strategies they have learnt in their lesson. For example:

To successfully read a longer article quickly, we should:
- ☐ Check the headline and photos and predict what we think the story is about.
- ☐ Take a moment to think about what we know about this topic.
- ☐ Not read every word in the article.
- ☐ Read the introduction in full.
- ☐ Read the first and last line of each paragraph.

In this scenario, there are no linguistic criteria but there is still clear guidance against which learners can assess their success. Without success criteria, skills can be more challenging for both learners and teachers to assess and notice progress with as they are often more intangible than systems lessons focused on items of vocabulary or the use of a grammar point. In language-focussed lessons, there is often a clear correct or incorrect answer. Success criteria in receptive skills development provide the tools both learners and teachers need to assess their success and to discuss how this skill could be applied to other lessons and to their lives.

See **Part B, Chapter 5** for lesson ideas and examples of Overt Teaching in skills tasks.

Key principle 5: Creating prime conditions for dialogic feedback

So far in the lesson, the teacher has established and discussed what the objective of the lesson is, and learners know what success looks like and have personalised that success, clearly communicating their own expectations. With guidance and feedback, the learners are on track for success. Providing effective feedback is the next step.

One particular challenge for many teachers is monitoring learner output. At any one time, how many learners can you realistically monitor? If we assume that we can actively listen to a single group, then (depending on the size of our classes and groups) there might be up to 90% of learner output that teachers are missing out on. Once we introduce personalised success criteria, another challenge is remembering which criteria each learner has chosen to focus on, as this is what they would most benefit from receiving feedback on. For smaller class sizes this is already challenging, but for larger groups it becomes impossible to achieve.

Peer feedback

One solution to these challenges is empowering learners to self-assess and give feedback to their peers. In 1960 Graham Nuthall began researching the effect various teaching practices had on the outcomes of learners by recording classroom conversations. He continued until 2000 and then passed away in 2004. His research was published posthumously in 2007 and is 'increasingly being seen as a seminal text for understanding learning' (Tishauser, 2019). In this study, one of the longest of its kind that has ever been carried out, Nuthall (2007) found that it was peers who provided 80% of the verbal feedback in a classroom, meaning that it was learners and not the teacher who were providing the majority of feedback in lessons. As our learners are not the English language experts in the classroom, we cannot say for certain how valuable all of this feedback might be, but that does not negate its presence or importance. Valuable or not, the fact remains that peer feedback is a regular feature of lessons and we should therefore work with it, giving learners the tools they need to give valuable, constructive feedback. As Black and Wiliam (1998, p9) discuss in their *Inside the Black Box* series, 'pupils are generally honest and reliable in assessing both themselves and one another.'

Peer feedback is sometimes avoided by teachers. It may not be constructive or useful, perhaps focussing only on the content as opposed to the language or skills used. For example, a learner tells a story and then hears the following feedback:

- 'It was a very good story.'
- 'I haven't been to that city, I should go.'
- 'Your pronunciation was not very clear. I could not understand very well.'

As you can see, these are probably not the most useful examples of feedback. The first is too vague, making no reference to why the story was good or what steps could be taken to make it even better. The second is content-based, commenting only on what has been said and not the level of success that has been obtained. One could argue that this kind of feedback would be more natural in the real world and is therefore relevant. However, it all depends on the aim of the feedback, which comes back to effective instructions. Learners must know what is expected of them both in terms of production and feedback. The final piece of feedback is perhaps the one we most wish to avoid as it is quite subjective and the storyteller may take offense at it.

The issue in each of these scenarios is that the learners have not been give the tools to give effective feedback. Feedback is typically an area that teachers spend whole sessions discussing during training courses, that schools hold regular training and standardisation sessions on, and that feature regularly in conferences. Teachers know it takes time and training to learn how to give effective feedback, but learners are asked to do so without the benefit of this input. Effective success criteria give our learners the parameters with which to judge learner output more objectively and constructively.

Mini monitors

Pair work is a common interaction pattern for conversation tasks in the language classroom. However, if learners are expected to focus on their own output, they are less likely to be able to monitor what their peers are saying. Moving to groups of three learners allows two learners to converse while a third monitors and gives feedback. It also allows the other members of the group to challenge the feedback as there are now two potential listeners, as is demonstrated in this conversation:

Learner A: Your story was very good. You used the past simple for your main actions, but I didn't hear you use the past continuous to start the story.

Learner B: I thought I did.

Learner C: You did. You said something like 'I was walking in the street when I saw someone.'

Learner A: Oh, sorry! I didn't hear you. How would that work?

With a teacher monitoring and three learners using success criteria to give and discuss feedback, we create a system with more checks and balances, leading to negotiated feedback. By participating in this kind of activity regularly, learners gradually improve their feedback skills. There is also more output for the teacher, who can now monitor both the task and the feedback discussion, and intercede with advice, clarifications or corrections.

To learn more, see **Part B, Chapter 4, 'Setting up effective peer-to-peer feedback'**.

Reflecting on success

It's important to remember that '...pupils can only assess themselves when they have a sufficiently clear picture of the targets that their learning is meant to attain' (Black and Wiliam, 1998, p9). At the time of writing, David is learning to drive (quite late in his life!) and every time he performs a manoeuvre, his instructor asks him how he thinks it went. David knows what success looks like: being able to pull up beside a vehicle and reverse parallel park behind it in a single manoeuvre. After every attempt he's able to dissect his performance, identify where he went wrong and make a decision about what he's going to do differently next time. His instructor can then quickly and easily comment on his reflection and provide any further tips for upgrading his performance.

Feedback is crucial to the learning process. It can come from a number of sources and still be effective. In that car, David and his knowledge and experience are resources which the instructor exploits to help him develop. The same applies in the language classroom. Our learners are one of our greatest resources. With the right guiding questions and prompts, we can enable them to reflect on their own performance and make decisions about what they will try next.

With time, support and practice, learners will become adept at reflecting on success but at first they will need class time which is devoted to helping them to create reflection questions from their success criteria. For example, imagine the objective of a lesson is 'To be better able to tell engaging stories about an event' and one of the success criteria is 'Using the past continuous to set the scene at the beginning of the story (e.g. 'I was walking down the street when...')'. Reflection questions for this particular criterion might be:

1. Did I set the scene at the beginning of the story?
2. Did I use past continuous to do this?
3. What would I do differently next time?

In this example, there are two aspects to a single criterion so learners can reflect on how well they achieved both aspects and what they will do to improve on their stories.

Practical ideas for creating reflection questions from success criteria can be found in ⏩ **Part B, Chapter 4, 'Reflecting on success'**.

When encouraging reflection, it might seem like this is a task best carried out by an individual learner and then discussed with the teacher. However, one challenge with this which Black and Wiliam (1998) point out is that it can be ineffective if teachers ask learners directly to give answers immediately and do not allow enough time for them to think first. Carrying out the reflection discussion in pairs or groups of three first gives the learners time to consider and discuss their own success, allows other learners to comment and support them and gives the teacher more output to monitor and more opportunities for the discussion of learning. In our experience, learners benefit from hearing each other's reflections and begin to consider areas they might not otherwise have done.

The teacher's role in feedback

If learners are able to self-assess and give feedback effectively, what role does the Overt Teacher play? Are they merely facilitators of learning, enabling the discussions but not taking part? Definitely not! Teachers are first and foremost *teachers*, which suggests an active role in the teaching, and therefore learning, process. Enabling our learners to give feedback does not in any way negate the need for a teacher to be present. What it does instead is create multiple layers of feedback:

- Layer 1: learners self-assess and give peer feedback
- Layer 2: teacher feedback to groups
- Layer 3: final whole-class feedback

The first layer of feedback following an activity is peer-to-peer, entirely focused on those learners' chosen success criteria. Meanwhile, the teacher can move around the classroom giving feedback to groups and discussing the feedback they've given each other, gradually informing themselves and expanding on what they noted from their own monitoring. This then leads to a final whole-class feedback stage where the teacher gives praise and suggests upgrades based on the success criteria.

Repetition

David was once in first aid training and he attempted to raise the chin and head of the dummy to the correct level in order to clear the airways. He did not achieve this as effectively as he could have done and was told this by the trainer, who quickly moved on to the next person. This left David with a feeling of frustration, knowing that he would not get another chance to be successful, knowing that he could now see where he had gone wrong and what he should try differently next time. However, he never got the opportunity to repeat what he was practising and get feedback on his (hopefully!) improved performance. To this day, David would not feel confident to step forward in a situation requiring first aid.

Informed repetition is what leads to improvement. The language classroom is no different. To learn language, we need to encounter it several times; to develop skills we need the opportunity to practice them again and again. It is important therefore that we build this repetition into our lesson planning, remembering though that practice alone is not sufficient. Hattie and Clarke (2019, p17) discuss the idea of 'deliberate practice' which they describe as not merely repeating the exact same exercise or activity but instead practice with 'deliberate teaching, feedback and success criteria'. With this in mind, repetition becomes a key part of the learning discussion and process.

Let's consider the average learner moving into a major communicative task. It can be a daunting prospect with a lot of different factors for them to consider:

- **Content:** They have to consider the content they are expected to create. Should they share personal information or create something new? Is this a real or imagined scenario?
- **Task:** There is always the possibility that they didn't fully understand the instructions and are unsure of where they are supposed to be in the room, or who they should speak to, or how what notes they need to make.
- **Personality:** Learners have their own personalities to consider. Coming across as yourself in a second language is not always easy; it takes some thought to work your humour or sensitivity or beliefs into what you say.

These are all major factors, without even considering the newly learnt language or skills the learners are expected to demonstrate as part of the task. Very often the first time a communicative task happens, learners focus on content and ignore the language and skills they have just been taught. This can be frustrating as teachers because it gives us very little to provide feedback on. That is unless we accept that this will happen, work it into our plans, and plan for repetition. Once content and personality issues are out of the way, learners can focus on carrying out the same or a similar task but this time meeting the success criteria that have been negotiated.

The question then becomes, is one repetition enough? How many repetitions is reasonable? It really depends on the task and how well the learners meet the success criteria, but there is usually room for improvement. This might be a slight upgrade or it might be the addition of an entire new layer of challenge, with additional success criteria. Just because a learner has chosen their criteria for success, it doesn't mean that this is their ceiling for the lesson. These criteria can be renegotiated constantly as the lesson develops and learners understand better what they are capable of achieving.

To learn more about this, see ⏩ **Part B, Chapter 4: Feedback, reflection and repetition**.

Summary

As Part A has laid out, there is a clear thread stretching from aims and objectives to success criteria, and all the way to feedback, reflection and repetition, with each informing the next. These give us our five key principles of Overt Teaching:

Key principles of Overt Teaching

1. An Overt Teacher believes learners should know **what they are learning**.
2. An Overt Teacher believes learners should know **why they are learning it**, namely how the things they are learning can be applied to their lives outside the classroom.
3. An Overt Teacher believes that a learner should be **involved in discussions about what they are learning**.
4. An Overt Teacher believes learners will benefit from **choosing and discussing their own levels of success**.
5. An Overt Teacher believes that learners should be involved in **dialogic feedback about their success**.

These principles can be applied to any lesson. If this is done effectively, they will enable teachers to carry out overt discussions of learning and learner progress throughout their lessons. Part B will introduce practical tips and ideas on how to implement the principles in your lessons.

B

Introduction

The aim of Part B is to provide you with practical tasks to help you to take a more Overt Approach to the discussion of learning, introducing it into your language classroom and promoting its importance. If you used the reflection questionnaire in the introduction to Part A, you will already have reflected on which areas of your teaching are possibly more overt or covert at the moment. If not, you may wish to go back to the questionnaire now. Depending on where you are on your journey to becoming an Overt Teacher, you may wish to start at the beginning of this section and work your way through the activities or you can choose to focus on specific areas of that you have identified.

Organisation of Part B

Each of the chapters in Part B addresses the different aspects of Overt Teaching discussed in depth in Part A. They start with a brief overview of what can be found in the chapter and then move on to practical examples and tasks. There are five chapters:

1. Know your why
2. Aims and objectives
3. Success criteria
4. Feedback, reflection and repetition
5. Skills development

The chapters are divided into sections, helping you to gradually become more overt in your approach, one area at a time. Each section is divided into four parts: **Tips**, **Task**, **Try it out**, and **Take it further**.

Tips

In this section, we will review and expand upon some of the relevant information from Part A. We will share practical classroom examples and provide you with tips to help you take a more Overt Approach in your lessons.

Task

Here you will be given a task based on an example from a classroom setting, giving you the opportunity to try out and reflect on the Tips. At the end of the book there is an **Answer Key** containing reflections on these tasks so that you can check your ideas and continue your development. Some of the Tasks ask you to look at a specific lesson plan, which you can find just before the **Answer Key**.

Try it out

At this point it's time to take what you've learnt into your lessons. Here, you will find step-by-step ideas you can immediately put into practice.

Take it further

These extension tasks help you to develop this area further, expanding on the tasks you've already tried. We will give you practical ideas for continuing your development in this area.

Chapter 1

Know your why

Introduction

As discussed in Part A, the first two key principles of Overt Teaching are that an Overt Teacher believes learners should know what they are learning and why they are learning it. In the language classroom, we are very often focused on completing the task at hand without considering why this task might be important for learners, or why we have organised it in a particular way. When it comes to materials, it is not always immediately clear to learners or even to us as teachers why something has been included in a piece of material. In this chapter you'll learn to ask the key question about an activity: Why are we doing this?

This is a skill that will take time to develop but the activities which follow will help you on that journey. Understanding why an activity is important will not only help you to plan your lessons, decide which activities need more focus, and write effective aims and objectives but also to hold overt discussions with your learners about their English-language learning.

In this chapter, you will find the following tasks:

- **Knowing your material:** How to analyse materials and coursebooks to uncover the reason behind an activity.
- **Ask yourself why:** How to reflect upon why you organise your lesson the way you do.
- **Why did the writer write this sentence:** How to help learners analyse language in context.
- **Why did they do that? Using successful people as models:** How to analyse how people speak so that you can better discuss speaking skills with your learners.
- **Discussing the learners' 'why':** How to keep the learning discussion focused on your learners' goals, helping them to see the relevance of what they are learning.

Knowing your material

Tips

Every activity in published materials was included by the writers for a clear reason. The Overt Teacher understands and discusses those reasons with their learners so they get the most from each activity. Luckily, lessons and coursebooks tend to follow a similar layout regardless of the writer or series, and activities tend to have similar reasons behind them. Knowing common reasons for activities will give you the tools you need to decide which ones to focus on in your lessons, which ones you can give less importance to and which ones to discuss overtly with your learners.

You can use these tips to decide on the possible reason for an activity:

- How will this activity help the learner achieve the lesson objective?
- What information will this activity give the teacher?
- Does this activity practise or develop a particular sub-skill, such as writing topic sentences in paragraphs?
- Does this activity practise or develop a particular learning skill, such as using dictionaries effectively?
- Look at the activities before and after this one. Does this activity add to the previous one or prepare for the next one in some way?

For example, learners are learning to give directions in this lesson:

Focus on language

Work in pairs. Read the conversation below. Discuss questions 1-4.

1. How does Speaker A stop someone politely to ask for directions?
2. What language point does Speaker B use to give directions?
3. How does Speaker A check the directions they heard?
4. What vocabulary for directions does Speaker A use?

(A) Excuse me. Do you know where Bistro Café is?

(B) Of course. Keep going down this road and then turn left at the bottom. It's next to the shopping centre.

(A) Sorry, was that left at the end of this road?

We can ask the questions above and decide on the possible reasons for the inclusion of this activity in the lesson:

- To provide a model for the target conversation.
- To practise analysing language in context.
- To revise / teach the target language in context.

Task

1. Look at the materials for Lesson 1: Talking about friends, for intermediate (B1) learners.
2. Write possible reasons for the inclusion of each activity in the lesson. There may be more than one reason for each activity.
3. Look at the **Answer Key** to check your ideas.

Activity	Reason(s)
A. Introduction	
B. Learn by reading	
C. Focus on vocabulary	
D. Focus on language	
E. Preparing to speak	
F. Speaking	
G. How did you do?	

Try it out

1. Copy a lesson from your coursebook, or other materials you use.
2. Next to each activity, write possible reasons for the inclusion of that activity on the page.
3. To check your ideas, compare them with a colleague. Alternatively, read the teachers book as it often explains the reasons for key activities.

Take it further

Once you're confident you know the reason behind each activity in your materials, you can make more informed decisions. For each activity in your lesson, ask yourself the questions below:

- Is it important for my learners to know the reason behind this activity?
- Is it worth spending lesson time discussing this reason?
- Is this activity necessary for my learners?

Use your answers to make decisions about which activities to focus on, which to avoid and which to spend time overtly discussing with your learners.

Ask yourself why

Tips

As a teacher, you are a valuable resource. Before your lesson, you plan what you and the learners are going to do, and throughout your lesson you make decisions about how to do it. Perhaps you plan to begin with a conversation about the topic of the lesson and then in the lesson you decide who to pair with whom. Perhaps you plan to teach a specific language point and then in the lesson you decide to skip it and focus on something else instead. Perhaps you plan to do a vocabulary matching exercise and, in the class, you decide to monitor and see which questions your learners are getting right or wrong. You constantly make decisions.

The question is why. Why do you decide to get learners to work individually or in pairs? Why do you decide not to teach a particular language point? Why do you decide to monitor to check learners' answers? We might know that we should monitor or put learners in pairs but we're not completely sure why we're doing it. If we don't know why, we can't discuss our reasons with learners.

Task

Read activities A-D, focussing on the sections in **bold**. The teacher might include the activity in the lesson for any of the reasons in the 'Why' column. However, one reason could generally be considered more important than the other two. Choose which one (1, 2, or 3) and decide why it might be the most useful reason to include this activity in the lesson.

Look at the **Answer Key** to check your ideas.

Activity	Why
A. In the lesson, the learners are going to read an article on fast fashion. **The teacher begins the lesson with some discussion questions on fashion and shopping habits**.	1) To engage learners in the topic and see what they know. 2) To warm learners up. 3) To get learners speaking English.
B. Before they read the article, **the learners look at the picture and the headline and try to guess what the article will be about**.	1) To practise their prediction skills. 2) Because it mirrors how we read articles outside the class. 3) To practise talking about pictures.
C. After they read, the teacher sets the learners some gist reading questions. **They put them in pairs to check their answers** before looking at them together.	1) To give learners speaking practice. 2) To let learners check their ideas before they share as a class. 3) To let learners learn from their partners.
D. The learners are working on a vocabulary matching exercise based on the article. **The teacher stands up and walks from group to group monitoring.**	1) To check the learners are completing the right exercise. 2) To make sure the learners are not using their phones. 3) To check which questions learners need extra support with.

Try it out

1. Write out the key stages for your next lesson, with space after each stage to write notes.
2. During the lesson, make notes of the decisions you made during that stage. Consider:
   a. How you gave instructions (e.g. written or spoken, checked or not checked)
   b. The groups you chose (e.g. pairs, 3s, etc.)
   c. How you set up the seating
   d. What you monitored for while learners were working
   e. What feedback you gave learners
3. After the lesson look back over your notes and consider why you made each decision. Use the prompt 'I took this action because…' to write your reasons.
4. Reflect on your reasons. Would you make the same decision again in a similar situation?

Take it further

You are a valuable resource but so are the learners. After major activities, ask learners why they thought you set it up as you did. We have found that gradually raising learners' awareness of why you are doing what you do as a teacher increases their engagement in lessons. Their increased awareness of the learning process allows them to have more effective discussions about this process.

Why did the writer write this sentence?

Tips

In his book *Teaching Grammar: From Rules to Reasons*, Danny Norrington Davies makes the argument for a more inductive approach to grammar learning, in which learners use guiding questions to work out the rules for the use of a particular language for themselves, using an example of the language in context. While this is a common approach to language learning and one that can be seen in many coursebooks these days, Danny goes even further, believing that by focusing on the writer or speaker, the genre and the context of a text, learners can discern why *this* person produced *this* piece of language in *this* instance, giving them a better idea of how the language can be used.

This is an incredibly useful skill for both learners and teachers to develop. The Overt Teacher can discuss grammar rules with their learner, but perhaps more importantly, they can discuss why a piece of language was used by a particular writer or speaker in a particular way. It is in this discussion that we can help our learners to see how the rules they learn in the classroom can be put into practice in their real lives.

Task

1. Read the text message between two housemates and answer the questions:
   - Why did the first housemate use the future continuous?
   - What do you think the first housemate will ask next?
2. Look at the ⏩ **Answer Key** to check your ideas.

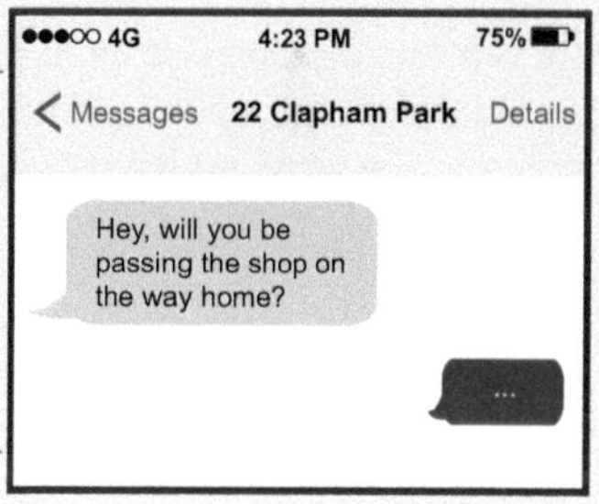

Try it out

1. Choose a listening task you will use with your learners.
2. Before the lesson, listen to the audio and read along with the transcript (if provided).
3. Choose examples of language points being used in the audio and ask yourself the following questions:
   a. Why did the speaker use this language point in this situation?
   b. What are they trying to communicate or achieve?
   c. Which words did the speaker stress?
   d. Why did they stress them? What intonation did they use? Why did they use it?
4. Compare your ideas with a colleague if possible.
5. In class, ask your learners the same questions and compare your answers with them. This will reveal their understanding of the language points and the discussion may even reveal ideas you hadn't considered.

Take it further

Our family and friends are an incredible resource when developing the skill of analysing language and why it has been used. Look back through messages you've received and consider why specific language points were used. Over time, you'll develop this skill to a point where you can hold more spontaneous discussions with your learners about language, helping them to understand the many uses of the language points they encounter.

Why did they do that? Using successful people as models

Tips

Throughout this book we refer to aims as the various stages which need to be mastered in order to successfully complete an objective. In **Part B, Chapter 2**, you will practise wording these effectively but first you need to be able to look at an objective and decide what exactly a learner would need to master in order to fully achieve it; what language points, vocabulary chunks and skills would help them to be successful in this lesson.

The important thing to remember is that you, your colleagues, the people you watch on television or listen to, and the writers whose work you read are often successful. They are walking, talking models of success. When considering a lesson objective and wondering what the aims might be, the first question to ask yourself is what would I do if I was in this situation?

In this example lesson, the objective is 'To be better able to have a discussion about global issues.' If Mark and David were having a discussion on global issues, we would:

- Use a range of vocabulary related to the global issues we're discussing.
- Agree and disagree with each other using various phrases.
- Explain possible actions/inactions and their consequences.
- Interrupt each other politely.
- Use our facial expressions and body language to convey our agreement / disagreement.
- Buy thinking time so we can formulate our thoughts.

Once you know what a successful person would do in this situation, you can consider which of these would be appropriate to teach to your learners and how you could do this.

Task

1. You have an upper intermediate (B2) group. The objective of your lesson is to be able to have a discussion on global warming, similar to the one we considered in Tips.
2. Write 3-5 aims for your lesson using the ideas in Tips or your own ideas.
3. Look at the **Answer Key** to check your ideas.

Try it out

1. Look at the objective for your next lesson.
2. Write down everything you would do or that you have seen others do in this situation.
3. Write notes on the language points, the vocabulary chunks, and the skills you would use in this situation.
4. Assess your list and decide which are appropriate to teach your learners.
5. Use this to write your aims. See **Part B, Chapter 2** if you need help with this.

Take it further

The more aware you are of what a successful person would do in a situation, the easier it is to decide what to teach your learners. For example, when speaking, think about why you speak in a certain way. When you agree with someone, do you hold your head in a specific way? Do you raise your chin slightly when you disagree or are unsure? Do you nod when you're showing interest, or do you make noises of interest and agreement? If English is not your first language, do you show interest differently in English and your language? The more you consider these questions, the more able you will be to instruct your learners on effective communication.

Discussing the learners' 'why'

Tips

Depending on the context you teach in, your learners may or may not have a clear idea of their own English-language needs. For example, if you are teaching seven-year-olds, they will most likely not yet be aware of their life goals and how a knowledge of English will impact that. However, many learners will have a clear idea of why they are learning English and this will affect how they judge the relevance of a particular lesson or task. The Overt Teacher recognises the importance of this information and discusses it regularly throughout their lessons to help learners see the importance of tasks.

Task

1. Read the profiles of Learners A-C and the lesson aims and objective below. Answer questions i-iv.
   i. Why might some of these learners feel the lesson objective is not relevant for them?
   ii. How could you help them see the relevance of the objective?
   iii. Why might some of the learners feel the pronunciation stage is not relevant?
   iv. How could you help them see the importance of the pronunciation stage?
2. Look at the **Answer Key** to check your ideas.

Lesson aims and objective:

Today we are going to:
- Listen to friends talk about their plans for the weekend.
- Learn vocabulary for social activities.
- Learn to use 'be going to' to talk about plans.
- Learn to use 'will' to make decisions about plans.
- Focus on pronunciation: Learn the fast speech forms of 'will' and 'be going to'.

So that you can:
- Speak about your plans for the weekend.

Learner profiles:
- **Learner A:** This learner is learning English for their job. They work in a multinational company where the main language of communication is English. They are German but their colleagues are mostly Japanese and Taiwanese.
- **Learner B:** This learner is mostly interested in learning English to travel and socialise.
- **Learner C:** This learner is from Taiwan and wants to be able to communicate with their son-in-law from Brazil. English is their shared language. They want to be able to enjoy movies and TV shows together in English.

Try it out

1. Begin your lesson by asking learners why they are learning English. Elicit some examples to encourage them to be as specific as possible.
2. Communicate the aims and objective of the lesson.
3. Give learners time in small groups to discuss the relevance of each part of the lesson to their learning goals.
4. Move between groups, where necessary helping learners to understand how the aims and objective might apply to their learning goals. For example, a learner might not immediately see how a lesson on explaining a recipe would help them become a tour guide. However, if this lesson includes the skills of instruction giving and checking understanding, this could be very useful for a tour guide.

Take it further

Gather learners' goals and display them in the classroom (if possible). Refer to them each lesson to keep learners focused on their goals and help them to see how their lessons help them to reach those goals. It can be a good idea to ask learners to reflect on their goals periodically to see if they have been achieved and new goals need to be set, or if they need to be edited slightly. A learner's goals might change regularly, and it is important for both the learner and the teacher to know what they are.

Chapter 2

Aims and objectives

Introduction

Aims and objectives are the scaffolding that holds up the entire learning discussion in an Overt Teacher's lessons. When written effectively, they can be used to help learners see what they are learning, why they're learning it, what success looks like and how all of it is relevant for their lives outside the classroom. They are the blueprints for your lesson and with them you can place your learners firmly at the centre of the learning discussion.

The challenge for the teacher is writing them in such a way that they can be easily accessed and understood by their learners; that they are focused without being too narrow; and that there is enough information there to encourage discussion without overwhelming. The tasks in this chapter will help you learn to do just that.

In this chapter, you will find the follow tasks:

- **Writing real-world objectives:** How best to word your objectives so that they reflect the real lives of your learners.
- **Writing decontextualised objectives:** How to write objectives that are focused but not too narrow.
- **Writing effective aims:** How to word your aims so they are clear and informative.
- **Formatting aims and objectives:** How to organise your aims and objectives so that learners can easily access and understand them.
- **Beginning the learning conversation:** How to use aims and objectives to promote the discussion of learning throughout your lesson.
- **Keeping the conversation going:** How to encourage learners to practise the objective outside the classroom.

Writing real-world objectives

Tips

When writing an effective objective, it is important to consider the lesson as a whole. The goal is to help learners to see how this lesson can be applied to their lives. Ask yourself the following questions:

- What are the real-life implications of your lesson for your learners?
- What will they be better able to do in their lives?
- Which of their needs does this objective meet?

It is possible that there might be two clear objectives in a lesson, depending on the time you have with your learners. Once you can answer the questions above, it's time to word the objective. To make it accessible to learners, it's important to write it to them directly, in language appropriate for their level. Consider beginning with the sentence prompt:

- By the end of the lesson, you will be (better) able to...
- Once it is written, the effectiveness of the objective can be assessed using the questions below and any edits can be made based on this assessment.
- Is it written in learner-friendly language?
- Does it speak directly to the learners?
- Does it contain a real-world objective that might be relevant to learners?

Task

Look at three possible objectives (A-C) for an intermediate (B1) level IELTS class. Use the Tips to assess how effective they might be. Look at the **Answer Key** to check your ideas.

Possible objectives

A. By the end of the lesson, you will be able to complete writing task 2 in IELTS.
B. By the end of the lesson, the learners will be better able to use negative inversion.
C. By the end of the lesson, you will be better able to organise your paragraphs so that they are easier for a reader to understand.

Try it out

1. For your next lesson, prepare to write your real-world objective by considering these questions:
   a. What are the real-life applications of this lesson for these learners?
   b. What will these learners be better able to do in their real lives?
   c. Which of their needs does this lesson meet?
2. Write your real-world lesson objective.
3. Use these questions to assess your objective:
   a. Is the language appropriate for these learners?
   b. Does it speak directly to these learners?
   c. Does it contain a real-world objective that is relevant to these learners?
   d. Is one real-world objective enough for this lesson?
4. If necessary, edit, add, or rewrite your objective before assessing it again.

Take it further

In all of the questions used to assess objectives in Try it out, the key word is 'learners'. As discussed in **Part A**, it is important to communicate objectives to learners. However, as with many teaching skills, writing effective objectives is a skill that needs to be improved over time. Involving learners in this process can be valuable. Use these tasks to begin involving your learners in this process:

1. Write your real-world objective and communicate it to your learners.
2. Give them time to assess the objective using the assessment questions above.
3. Discuss as a group whether or not the learners feel the objective is relevant to them and applicable to their lives.

Writing decontextualised objectives

Tips

When discussing learning intentions, Hattie and Clarke (2019, p54) argue that they should be decontextualized, giving the example of the difference between 'Learning to design a poster for a holiday in St Lucia' and 'Learning to design a poster'. The latter is decontextualised, and therefore transferrable to other situations: the learners can apply the skills they've learnt to any poster. The former is contextualised, making a poster specific to St Lucia, which is a requirement that may not arise again for these learners.

To ensure that lesson objectives are not overly contextualised, it can be useful to word them with the focus on the transferrable skill or conversation and then give the specific lesson context as an example. For example, the aim of an activity where learners read an article then discuss its content could be communicated as:

- **Contextualised:** Read an article on art and summarise it for your partner.
- **Decontextualised:** Practise summarising what you've read (e.g. articles).

It is clear from the decontextualised aim that a particular skill is being practised in a single context, but could be applied to many others. This can then lead to a discussion of what other contexts this skill can be applied to and how learners might apply it to their lives.

Task

1. Read the contextualised aims and objective in the table. Where possible, rewrite them to be decontextualised, so that learners will be able to see how they can apply to other situations. Note that it's not always possible to decontextualise an aim or objective!
2. Look at the **Answer Key** to check your ideas.

Contextualised objectives	Decontextualised objectives
Today we are going to: ▸ Listen to a discussion about crime and punishment. ▸ Learn vocabulary to discuss crime and punishment. ▸ Learn to share and support your opinions. ▸ Learn to agree / disagree. ▸ Learn to outline your reasons for disagreeing. **So that you can:** ▸ Discuss crime and punishment and agree/ disagree with your partners.	

Try it out

1. Look at your objectives for upcoming or previous lessons. Use the questions below to reflect on them.
   a. Is this objective only useful in a single context?
   b. Is it clear how this objective could be applied to other situations apart from the one in the lesson?
2. Rewrite your objective if necessary. Ensure that:
   a. The focus is on the transferrable skill or conversation.
   b. The context is presented as an example.

Take it further

1. Identify activities that practise or test a skill in your lesson materials.
2. Write decontextualised task aims for the skills activities.
3. Communicate them to your learners and discuss how this skill could be applied outside the classroom.

Writing effective aims

Tips

When planning a lesson, it can be tempting for teachers to begin with what they want to cover in that lesson. However, this is probably not the most beneficial starting point for learners. Whether planning from a coursebook or creating a lesson from scratch, the process should be the same. The first step to writing effective aims that can lead to the effective discussion of learning is to be clear about the objective. This communicates what you want your learners to achieve, what you want them to be able to do better by the end of the lesson. Once this has been established, you can work backwards and consider which aims would best achieve this objective for these learners.

When writing aims, it is important to consider not only curriculum needs and what the learners need to learn, but also what prior knowledge they are bringing to the classroom. This can help you assess whether you need to introduce something for the first time, revise it, or if you can assume learners already know it. It can also be helpful to consider cultural aspects. For example, if you're teaching learners to have a group discussion about a global topic, are they all going to show they are listening in a similar way?

For more information on what an aim is and what information it should contain, see **Part A, Key principles 1, 2 and 3: Aims and objectives**.

Task

In this lesson, the objective is 'To be able to give a spoken review of a restaurant.' The lesson is for a pre-intermediate (A2/B1) level group. What could the aims of this lesson be? How would you word them? Write 3-5 aims. Look at the **Answer Key** to check your ideas.

Today we are going to:
- Aim 1:
- Aim 2:
- Aim 3:
- Aim 4:
- Aim 5:

So that you can:
- Give a spoken review of a restaurant you visited (e.g. to a friend)

Try it out

1. Think about your next lesson. Begin with your objective. Then write your aims.
2. Use the questions below to assess your aims:
   a. Is it clear how each aim leads towards the objective?
   b. Do your aims have clear signals to learners in the form of study verbs? (See **Part A, Key Principles 1, 2 and 3, 'Effective aims'** for more information about using study verbs.)
   c. Have you considered your learner's prior knowledge? Is this clear in the aims and choice of study verbs?
   d. Is it clear to learners what language and skills they will work on during the lesson?
3. Edit or rewrite your aims based on your assessment.

Take it further

Sometimes it can be challenging to figure out what your aims should be for a specific objective. If that happens, follow these steps to decide on your aims.

1. Complete the main task(s) you would like the learners to do. For example, record yourself having the conversation from the main activity or complete the writing, reading, listening task yourself (depending on what your objective is).
2. Reflect on the task you completed. Consider the questions below:
   a. What language and skills did you use to achieve the goal?
   b. Which of these skills and language items are relevant for your learners and their level?
   c. Use your answers to the question 2a and 2b to help you write your aims.
3. Use the guidance from Try it out to assess your aims.

Formatting aims and objectives

Tips

In Part A, we suggested four different formats for presenting aims and objectives. The key to all of them is consistency. Your learners need to be able to easily identify what they will be better at by the end of the lesson, and see clearly how they will achieve that. Writing aims that include language above your learners' levels, overusing metalanguage (the language of describing language, teaching and learning, such as grammar terminology), or frequently changing the layout you use can make it more difficult for learners to navigate aims and objectives. This can lead to wasting time, over-explaining or even disengagement from the learners.

Your format might be dictated by your institution, you might have some flexibility within a dictated framework or you may have complete freedom of choice in how your aims and objectives are presented. Whatever the situation, a successful format will:

- ☐ Be at the learners' level.
- ☐ Avoid irrelevant metalanguage.
- ☐ Provide clear signals as to what the objective is and what the aims are.

Task

Look at the materials for Lesson 1: Talking about friends, designed for intermediate (B1) level.

1. Choose the format which you will write your aims and objectives in.
2. Write the objective of the lesson.
3. Write your aims.
4. Assess your format using the checklist in Tips.
5. Look at the **Answer Key** to check your ideas.

See **Part B, Chapter 2, 'Writing real-world objectives' and 'Writing effective aims'** if you need help.

Try it out

It can be useful to involve your learners in developing the format you will use to display aims and objectives in your lessons. Try these steps to establish your format:

1. Choose a range of possible formats which you might want to use. Write the aims and objectives for your next lesson in each of these formats.
2. Display the different formats on the board. Give learners these discussion questions to help them decide which formats work best for them.
   a. In each format, is it clear what you will be better able to do by the end of the lesson?
   b. Is it clear what you will learn to help you be better able to do this?
   c. Which format did you find easiest to understand?

   Note: Depending on the level of your learners, you may choose not to use all of these questions or to reword them. For monolingual groups, you may wish to translate the questions into the learners' language as the aim is to choose the best format for the aims and objectives, rather than to test their English.
3. Based on the learners' feedback, choose the most effective format for the aims and objectives. Stick to that format in the future!

Take it further

1. Once a format has been established and your learners are used to it, they will be able to navigate aims and objectives without your support. Display your aims and objectives before the lesson starts, on the board or on screen, so learners can begin thinking about them before you start teaching.
2. A consistent format will be most effective if it is used by all teachers in an institution. Once you have established a format that works, you might want to negotiate with your colleagues and/or managers about making the format official at your institution.

Beginning the learning conversation

Tips

Now that we have a real-world objective and effective aims, written in a format that learners can easily understand, the question is how we can use them as more than just a tick list of the stages we have completed in the lesson. One common way to present aims and objectives to learners at the beginning of the lesson is as a monologue, with the teacher listing all of the aims and objectives and the learners listening passively. It's possible to go beyond this though: aims and objectives are the scaffolding that support the majority of the learning discussions you will have in your lesson. If written effectively, they can be discussed at the beginning of the lesson and returned to throughout. The goal of these discussions is to help your learners see the personal relevance of the lesson objective, how their own prior knowledge applies to this lesson, and which of the aims they will need to focus on. This conversation will help to frame all discussions on success later in the lesson as learners have already noticed which areas might be comfortable for them and which might be a challenge. Over time, this will help learners to notice their progress.

If your learners are used to engaging passively with lesson aims and the objective, they might struggle with a more active dialogue at first. As you have these discussions more often, this will change, as the learners gradually see the benefits and understand what is expected of them. When discussing the communication of the learning aims in a lesson, Black and Wiliam (1998, p10) write 'When pupils do acquire such overview, they then become more committed and more effective as learners.'

Task

Below are the lesson aims and objective for Lesson 1: Talking about friends, for intermediate (B1) level learners. How would you discuss these with your learners so that they:

- see the personal relevance of this objective?
- see how their own prior knowledge applies to this lesson?
- know which of the aims they will need to focus on?

Look at the **Answer Key** to check your ideas.

Today we are going to:

- Talk about our friends.
- Read people's comments about their friends.
- Learn vocabulary for talking about our relationship.
- Revise how to talk about how we met someone (using the past simple).
- Revise how to describe the length of a relationship (using the present perfect).
- Revise how to predict how people will get on (using 'will' and 'be going to').

So that you can:

- Describe your relationship with someone (e.g. before you introduce them to a friend).

Try it out

1. Write your lesson objective and aims.
2. Write questions to help learners discuss the objective and aims.
3. Display the lesson objective, aims and questions at the start of the lesson.
4. Give learners time to discuss the questions in pairs. Move between the groups and support learners where necessary.

Take it further

1. Before you try it out, carry out a discussion with your learners first to help them to understand why you are having a conversation about aims and objectives with them. Display the discussion questions below, giving them time to discuss the questions in small groups. Then discuss as a whole class. Finally, reveal your plan to discuss aims and objectives at the beginning of every lesson.
   - Do you always know what you are going to learn in your lessons?
   - Do you know why you are learning it?
   - Do you know how it will help you in your life?
   - Would you like to know these things before you begin your lesson?
2. Once your learners are used to discussing aims and objectives, you can display the discussion questions on the board before the class begins so your learners have time to consider them.

Keeping the conversation going

Tips

There is a lot going on for learners in the language classroom and even with the most effective aims, they can very quickly forget what they are working towards in the lesson overall and focus only on the task in front of them. This is not necessarily a problem but, as a learner, knowing how a task will help them in the future can lead to higher levels of engagement throughout the lesson. We therefore recommend that you don't only discuss the lesson aims and objective in the first few minutes of the lesson, but instead return to them regularly as the lesson progresses.

For more information on these discussions, see **Part A, Key principles 1, 2 and 3: Aims and objectives**.

Task

Look at Lesson 2: Spoken film reviews, for a pre-intermediate (A2/B1) group. It begins with the aims and objective of the lesson. Choose one later point in the lesson at which you might stop and discuss the aim of the upcoming task(s).

- What questions could you ask to keep learners focused on the lesson objective?
- What questions would show them how this activity will help them achieve this objective?

Write your questions. Look at the **Answer Key** to check your ideas.

Try it out

1. Look back at a lesson you have recently taught.
2. Identify moments when you could have stopped and helped your learners to reflect on the purpose of the activities you were carrying out. How might this have helped their focus?
3. Plan moments in your next lesson at which you will pause and discuss the purpose of the activities.
4. Plan your questions.
5. At the end of your lesson, reflect on any differences in the focus of your learners compared to your previous lesson.

Take it further

It can sometimes be hard to notice these moments yourself while you are teaching. Sometimes a second pair of eyes can be useful when developing a particular area. Ask a colleague or manager to observe you and identify any missed opportunities in your lesson in which learners lost focus on the objective and further discussion would have benefitted them. Alternatively (if your context allows it), you could record your lesson and watch it back to identify those moments yourself.

Chapter 3

Success criteria

Introduction

As discussed in **Part A**, the Overt Teacher believes learners will benefit from choosing and discussing their own levels of success. They believe that learners should be involved in dialogic feedback about their success. In order to have an effective dialogue, it is important that the teacher has put some scaffolding in place. This begins with effective aims and objectives as the first communication of what success might include. The next step is creating clear and effective success criteria to help learners to prepare for an activity and personalise success. In this chapter you will learn practical tips for the creation and wording of success criteria, allowing you to provide your learners with the support they need to choose, assess and discuss their own levels of attainment.

In this chapter, you will find the following tasks:

- **Using aims and objectives to create success criteria:** How to move from aims and objectives to success criteria.
- **Using a successful model to create success criteria:** How to use models to negotiate success criteria with learners.
- **Writing unsuccessful models:** How to use unsuccessful models to negotiate success criteria with learners.
- **Choosing success:** How to encourage your learners to choose and discuss success.
- **Visualising success:** How to use visual prompts to help learners to visualise success.

Using aims and objectives to create success criteria

Tips

An Overt Teacher ensures that learners are aware of what success looks like for the final activity of the lesson and involves them in the discussion of success. When first introducing success criteria, it is a good idea to refer back to your aims and objectives, as these are your first communication of success to your learners. It makes sense therefore that these aims and objectives inform your criteria for success.

For more information on the theory behind success criteria, please refer to **Part A, Key Principle 4: Choosing and discussing success**.

The creation of success criteria based on aims and objectives depends entirely on having already created and clearly communicated effective aims and objectives to your learners. If you are unsure of how to do this, we recommend working through Chapter 2 before proceeding.

When wording success criteria, it is a good idea to:

- Write them as a checklist so learners can self-assess themselves, ticking off criteria as they meet them.
- Word criteria as clearly as possible, including examples where relevant, so learners are aware exactly what is expected of them.
- Break an aim down into two or more criteria if it is complex.

Task

Read these aims and this objective for an intermediate (B1) story-telling lesson.

Today we're going to:

- Learn vocabulary chunks for activities on nights out.
- Learn to introduce a story (using 'You won't believe what happened last night.')
- Learn to begin a story (using the past continuous).
- Revise how to describe the main and background actions of a story (using past simple and past continuous).
- Revise common story linking words to make your story easy to follow.
- Learn to add background information to your story (using past perfect).

So that you can:

- Tell an engaging story of a fun night out.

Use the prompt and example below to write the remaining success criteria for this lesson.

Telling an engaging story of a night out means:
☐ Introducing your story using 'You won't believe what happened last night.'
☐ …

Look at the ⏩ **Answer Key** to check your ideas.

Try it out

1. Think back to a lesson in which you did not discuss with learners what success looks like for the final task. Reflect on how successful the learners were at achieving this task.
2. For your next lesson, ensure you have written effective aims and objectives, using the ideas in ⏩ **Part B, Chapters 1 and 2**.
3. Decide on the final task of the lesson. Use your aims and objective to write success criteria.
4. Give the criteria to learners before the final activity so they know what success would look like in that activity.
5. Use these reflection questions to compare this lesson to the one you considered in step 1.
   a. Did learners use the language and skills from each lesson in the final task?
   b. In each lesson did they use the language and skills successfully?
   c. Was it easier to give feedback in the second lesson? Why? / Why not?

Take it further

Once your learners are familiar with success criteria and how to word them, you can negotiate the criteria for success with them by displaying both the final task and the aims. As learners gradually get used to the process of criteria creation, you can just display the instructions for the final task on the board. Ask your learners to write their criteria for success in this task based on what they've learnt in the lesson. The lesson aims can then be displayed and referred to in order to check whether anything has been missed.

Using a successful model to create success criteria

Tips

Speaking or writing lessons in coursebooks and other published materials often include a model of the intended conversation or writing product earlier in the lesson. This could be a listening task in which the language and skills of the lesson are displayed or an example of the intended writing product. The Overt Teacher ensures that learners are aware that what they are seeing or listening to is an example of what they are working towards. Looking at these models again just before the final task can be an effective way of leading into it and ensuring everyone is clear what a good version looks like. When returning to these texts, use some or all of the guiding questions below to elicit success criteria from your learners.

1. Is this a successful example of _______?
2. What makes it successful?
3. What do the speakers use from today's lesson?
4. Find successful examples of everything we have learnt today.

The answers to these questions then help to form success criteria for the final task.

Task

In this lesson, elementary (A2) learners learn to introduce someone. This model is given at the beginning of the lesson. Examples are taken from the model throughout the lesson to teach learners the language they need.

> This is Shadi. He's my oldest friend. We went to school together. He's an engineer and he loves hiking and watching films.

1. Ask yourself questions 1 and 2 from Tips.
2. Use your answers and the model to help you to write 5 to 7 success criteria for a lesson with the objective 'Introducing a friend to one of your classmates'.
3. Look at the **Answer Key** to check your ideas.

Try it out

Next time your lesson materials include a good model, carry out the following steps:

1. When you get to the final task, ask your learners what a successful example will look like.
2. Elicit their ideas and then direct them to the model in the coursebook. Ask them to compare their ideas to the model.
3. Decide the final success criteria for the task together.

Take it further

As your learners get used to creating success criteria from models, you can introduce these discussions earlier in the lesson. For example, if there is a listening exercise at the beginning of the lesson which models a conversation learners will have in the final task, you can ask learners these questions (1-3) to begin conversations around success:

1. What was the point of this conversation?
2. How successful was this conversation?
3. What language did the speakers use to make it successful?

Success criteria can then be accumulated throughout the lesson, making it an ongoing conversation and helping learners to understand connections between different stages in the lesson.

Writing unsuccessful models

Tips

In the previous activity, we looked at generating success criteria from a successful model. However, an unsuccessful model presented before the final task can also give learners the opportunity to identify the key components of success. They can do this by highlighting what is problematic, inappropriate or missing.

As unsuccessful models aren't normally provided by coursebooks or resource books, you will probably need to write or record your own example. To do this, look at what has been taught in the lesson, look at the successful model and remove some or all of the factors leading to success. Here are two examples:

	Successful model	Unsuccessful model
Introducing a friend	This is Tadhg. He's an accountant. We met back in uni and have been friends ever since. You both have a lot in common. Tadhg is really into cooking and baking too.	This is Tadhg. I don't know what he does but he's lovely. You guys might get along.
Beginning an engaging story	I was walking down the road when suddenly I heard a strange noise. It was a low hum, but it was getting louder and louder. I started to feel nervous. It was dark and I'd never been in this area before. Then, out of nowhere, the aliens began to fall from the sky.	I was walking down the road and I heard something. It was quiet but got louder. I was nervous. It was dark. Then aliens fell from the sky.

Task

In this lesson, upper intermediate (B2) learners learn to write a formal email requesting information from a travel agency. The teacher communicates the lesson aims and the objective like this:

Today we're going to learn to write a formal email. The example we'll use is an email requesting information from a travel agency. First, we'll examine the basic organisation of an email, then we'll learn formal expressions for requesting information and formal expressions for opening and closing an email. Finally, we'll write emails to the school reception, requesting information about the upcoming school trip to Paris.

The example below is provided at the beginning of the lesson as a model. It is used to teach the various expressions learners will need to complete the final task.

1. Read the model.
2. Using the aims, objective, and successful model, write an unsuccessful version of the formal email from Jerry Flynn to Ms Molloy, requesting the same information.
3. Look at the **Answer Key** to see our version of an unsuccessful model.

Jerry Flynn Send

To cc bcc

Subject

Dear Ms Molloy,

I am writing to request further information about the trip to Glendalough, which is advertised on your website.

My first question is regarding accommodation. I was unclear if the price advertised included both accommodation for the evening as well as breakfast. I would be grateful if you could provide further information on what is included.

I was also wondering if you could inform me of any future dates once they have been decided. According to your website, there is currently no availability, but more dates will be advertised in the coming months. I would like to receive more information on this if possible.

Thanking you in advance. I look forward to hearing from you soon.

Kind regards,
Jerry Flynn

Try it out

1. Look through your materials for a successful model of a task.
2. Write your unsuccessful version of this model.
3. Use the reflection questions to assess your model:
   a. Does it still attempt the same basic purpose as the original model?
   b. Have you written enough for learners to notice what is missing?
   c. Have you chosen appropriate areas to edit? For example, if you have included spelling mistakes that aren't relevant to the lesson, it would become an editing activity for learners rather than an unsuccessful model.

Take it further

When the final task of a lesson is a speaking task, you can either give learners a written version of the conversation as an unsuccessful model or a recorded version. Ask colleagues or friends to record them saying the unsuccessful model. This allows you to expose learners to a greater range of speakers.

Using an unsuccessful model to create success criteria

Tips

In the previous activity, we looked at writing unsuccessful models. If presented before the final task, these models can help learners to identify the key components of success by highlighting what is problematic, inappropriate or missing. Discussion questions can guide learners in the creation of their own success criteria. For example:

- Is this a successful formal email to request information?
- What have we studied in today's lesson which could make it more successful?
- What would you change about this email to make it a formal information request?

Using unsuccessful models to spark the conversation around success has the dual benefits of reminding learners what they should include and developing their ability to assess their own success.

Task

This is the same lesson as in the previous activity, 'Writing successful models', where upper intermediate (B2) learners learn to write a formal email requesting information from a travel agency. As a reminder, the teacher communicates the lesson aims and the objective like this:

> Today we're going to learn to write a formal email. The example we'll use is an email requesting information from a travel agency. First, we'll examine the basic organisation of an email, then we'll learn formal expressions for requesting information and formal expressions for opening and closing an email. Finally, we'll write emails to the school reception, requesting information about the upcoming school trip to Paris.

1. Check the successful model in the previous task and the unsuccessful model in the **Answer Key** for 'Writing unsuccessful models'.
2. Write discussion questions you could give learners to help them create success criteria from the unsuccessful model.
3. Write success criteria for a formal email requesting information.
4. Look at the **Answer Key** to check your ideas.

Try it out

1. In your next lesson create an unsuccessful model of the final task.
2. Present it to your learners at the beginning of the lesson and ask them to discuss whether they think it is a good or bad example of what they are trying to achieve today.
3. Don't give them a final answer yet! Continue with your lesson.
4. Present the unsuccessful model again after all the input stages in the lesson. Give learners another chance to discuss how successful it is and why, based on what they have learnt.
5. Use this discussion to work with learners to create success criteria for the final task.

Take it further

As mentioned above, assessing unsuccessful models can help learners to develop their ability to assess their own work.

1. Begin your lesson with a task similar to the final task of the lesson (e.g. ask them to write a short email asking for information about a school trip).
2. Don't give feedback or check it. Instead, tell your learners that you'll return to it later on.
3. At the end of the lesson present your unsuccessful model and use it to establish the success criteria.
4. Give learners time to assess their own task from the beginning of the lesson and decide how it could be upgraded.
5. Get learners to complete the final task, using what they have learnt from assessing their own work.

This has the benefit of helping learners to clearly see their progress across the lesson as well as preparing them for what they want to include in the final task.

Choosing success

Tips

In any lesson, success will be different for each of your learners. The Overt Teacher uses success criteria to enable their learners to choose and discuss their own personal level of success. This might be a level-based decision in which a learner will choose not to attempt an entire more challenging criterion, or it could simply be the items of lexis that each learner chooses to use in their answers.

The learners should be involved in choosing their success criteria themselves, rather than the teaching deciding on the criteria for them. Having said that, it's important for the teacher to be able to guide the learners to select appropriate success criteria, which are both challenging but achievable.

For further information on this, please see **Part A, Key principle 4: Choosing and discussing success**.

Task

In this lesson, pre-intermediate (A2/B1) learners learn to discuss their outfits, with the following aims, objective and success criteria:

Today we are going to:	**Successfully having a conversation about someone's outfit means:**
Learn words / phrases to talk about clothes. ▸ Learn to ask questions about clothes using the past simple. ▸ Learn to hear/say 'did you' in fast speech. ▸ Revise telling stories using the past simple. ▸ Learn to compliment someone's clothes. **So that you can:** ▸ Have a conversation about someone's outfit.	☐ Beginning with a compliment. ☐ Using 3-5 clothing words/phrases from the lesson. ☐ Asking your partner a question about their outfit using past simple questions. ☐ Using the fast speech pronunciation of 'did you'. ☐ Telling the story of the outfit using past simple.

These are three of the learners in this lesson:

- **Learner A:** An elementary (A2) learner who was put in the group because there was no elementary class at the school.
- **Learner B:** An average pre-intermediate (A2/B1) learner.
- **Learner C:** A pre-intermediate (A2/B1) learner who is almost ready to move up to an intermediate (B1) class.

What do you think success would look like for each of these learners? Write personalised success criteria for them. Look at the **Answer Key** to check your ideas.

Try it out

1. In your next lesson, after creating success criteria with learners ask them to decide which of the criteria they are going to attempt in the final task.
2. Get learners to write down their personal success criteria with a tick box next to each one (as they are presented above).
3. After the task, give learners time to discuss how successful they were, ticking criteria they have achieved.
4. At this stage, it can be useful to repeat the task and give learners the chance to upgrade their responses to the task. See **Part B, Chapter 4, 'Setting up effective repetition'** for more advice on this.

Take it further

To help learners decide which of the success criteria they will include in their personal list, give them a traffic light system to assess each of the criteria:

- Green: I am totally comfortable with this.
- Orange: This is new but I think I can do this.
- Red: This is new and I am not sure I can do this yet.

Encourage learners to attempt all the green and orange criteria and to try one of the red ones.

Visualising success

Tips

It can be helpful to provide visual models to help learners to understand the level of success they are aiming to achieve. This can be particularly useful for younger learners or lower-level learners as they can refer to images without needing to have the language or awareness of learning to discuss the criteria. Having said that, it can be a useful tool across all levels and age groups. One way to help learners to understand different levels of success is the traffic light system mentioned on the previous page. Another idea is to use images of the different stages of building a house, which is what we will look at here.

In this example, the aims and objective of this lesson are:

Today we are going to:

- Learn to organise a cover email for a job application.
- Learn what information goes in each paragraph.
- Learn to write topic sentences for each paragraph.
- Learn to support your topic sentences with follow-up information.
- Learn to use linking words to help the reader follow your email.
- Learn to use formal language chunks throughout your email.

So that you can:

- Write a formal job application cover email.

Breaking down success into visual chunks might look like this, with later levels adding to earlier levels:

At this level...	The foundations	The rooms	The roof	The finished house

...the email:	☐ Is organised into appropriate paragraphs. ☐ Contains appropriate information in each paragraph.	☐ Has topic sentences for each paragraph. ☐ Contains appropriate formal language chunks throughout.	☐ Is easy to follow because of linking words.	☐ Has supporting information for each topic sentence.

One advantage of this approach is that it allows learners to easily communicate what they are aiming to achieve by just mentioning the visual representation by saying for example 'I'm going to try the house with the roof.' or 'I'm going to go for the finished house.' However, it might restrict individual choice of success criteria if the teacher has decided on the criteria for each of the levels in advance.

Task

1. Look at Lesson 2: Spoken film reviews, for pre-intermediate (A2/B1) level learners. Decide what success could look like for each of the four levels of the house in Tips.
2. Write your criteria for each level.
3. Look at the **Answer Key** to check your ideas.

Try it out

1. In your next lesson, present the images and discuss what each level represents.
2. Establish which criteria belong at each level. Note: this can be decided by you in advance or negotiated with your learners to help them grasp the concept of different levels of success.
3. Give learners time to decide which level they will aim to achieve in the task.
4. Use the different levels to help learners reflect on their success. See **Chapter 4** for more information on reflecting on success.

Take it further

The house works well as it has clear levels that learners can easily visualise. However, it is not the only possibility for a visual metaphor for success. Once the concept of visual levels has been introduced, ask learners to decide on and design other visuals. Young learners seem to particularly enjoy this activity. It is often very interesting to see what they come up with and can be set as a class project. For example, they could think about a cake, an ice-cream sundae or a pizza of success. They may choose to create a castle, vehicles or robots; whatever captures their imaginations and engages them in the concept of layers of success.

Chapter 4

Feedback, reflection and repetition

Introduction

It is hugely important that learners know what they are trying to achieve and know what success looks like for them. It is also important that they have the opportunity to practise the lesson objective and to try to improve, because none of us are perfect the first time we attempt a task. This is where feedback is essential. If learners are going to improve, they need to know what they need to improve, where they can upgrade their use of language, and generally how they can become even more successful. Feedback supplies this information.

But where does it come from? Feedback can of course come from the teacher but it can also come from classmates and from oneself. As long as the criteria for success have been communicated, reflection tasks allow learners to take ownership of their progress and to continue progressing without their teacher's presence. This feedback and reflection ensures that any future practice in this area is informed and drives progress.

In this chapter, you will find the following tasks:

- **Reflecting on success:** How to manage the reflection discussion.
- **Setting up effective peer-to-peer feedback:** How to help learners give feedback to their peers.
- **Setting up effective repetition:** How to include task repetition and give learners opportunities to improve.
- **Making homework meaningful:** How to set up repetition tasks outside class time.
- **Setting up effective post-lesson repetition:** How to help learners to repeat tasks beyond the lesson.
- **Post-lesson outcome mining:** How to reflect on relevant learning that emerged in the lesson.

Reflecting on success

Tips

In the Overt Classroom, both the teacher and the learners are expected to be aware of and discuss success. In the previous chapter, we examined how best to create success criteria to support that discussion. Learners will eventually become confident at using these criteria to reflect on past success and plan for future success, though this process is likely to take time and patience. When first using success criteria, you can help learners with this process by converting success criteria into reflection questions. A single criterion might have a number of aspects and might lead to multiple reflection questions.

For example, in a task requiring a learner to have a conversation one criterion for success is 'Showing interest with intonation and phrases from the lesson'. These questions might help learners to reflect by breaking this criterion down into its key factors for success:

1. Did I show interest when my partner was speaking?
2. When and how did I show interest?
3. When did I use intonation?
4. What phrases did I use?

Task

In this advanced (C1) lesson, the objective is 'By the end of the lesson, you will be better to discuss big issues in the news.' These are the success criteria for this task:

A successful discussion about big issues in the news means:

- ☐ Using an introductory phrase in the past simple to introduce a big issue you read.
- ☐ Using a range of collocations to describe big issues.
- ☐ Keeping the conversation going by commenting on what people say.
- ☐ Showing interest / surprise with phrases and intonation.

Use the criteria to write reflection questions for learners. Look at the **Answer Key** to check your ideas.

Try it out

1. Before the final task in the lesson, negotiate success criteria with your learners. See **Part B, Chapter 3** for more information on how to do this.
2. Display one of the success criteria on the board. Elicit possible reflection questions. Refine the questions as a group.
3. Give learners time in pairs to write their reflection questions. Display these question prompts to support them:
   a. Did I ... ?
   b. How did I ...?
   c. What did I use to ... ?
4. Elicit learners' ideas and finalise the reflection questions as a class.
5. Following the final task, display the reflection questions again. Give learners time to reflect on their success in small groups.

Take it further

Once learners are confident at reflecting effectively, they can begin to push themselves further. Add in these standard reflection questions to every discussion:

1. How challenging was this task for me?
2. Could I have attempted more of the criteria?
3. What will I do better next time?
4. How will I practise this outside the classroom?

By using these questions, you can encourage learners to see how this activity or lesson fits in as a step in their ongoing progression.

Setting up effective peer-to-peer feedback

Tips

Monitoring everything our learners produce in a speaking task can be incredibly challenging. Encouraging learners to reflect can help with this as they are essentially monitoring themselves. However, it can be challenging to hear our own errors. Sometimes a learner will believe they have been successful in an area when in fact they may not have been. Setting up peer-to-peer feedback creates an extra layer of monitoring.

Effective peer-to-peer feedback should be objective and constructive, and focused on success criteria. When setting up speaking tasks, ensure one learner in the group is not speaking, but has the role of monitoring. This means they are entirely focused on their partner(s) and are not thinking about their own production. It is important to make sure that the general success criteria and the speaker's personal criteria for success have been communicated to the monitor so that they know what to listen for.

Task

Imagine the following situation. Learners in an elementary (A2) group have learnt to talk about their plans for the weekend. The teacher puts learners in groups of three to talk about their plans. They tell the learners that they should give each other feedback after they speak. Learner A tells Learner B and C about her plans for the weekend and her partners give her this feedback:

Learner A: On Friday I will get pizza with my friend from Paris. We will go to a restaurant in town called Pizza Del Forno.

Learner B: Oh no. I do not like pizza, but I think your speaking is very good. I understand everything.

Learner C: I think 'will' is not correct here.

As you can see, Learners B and C do not have the tools they need to properly assess Learner A's output.

How could you set this activity up to support the learners in giving useful feedback? Write down 2-3 ideas. Look at the **Answer Key** to check your ideas.

Try it out

1. Before your final task, establish success criteria with your learners.
2. Explain that you want to help learners to give feedback to each other so they can help you in class and help each other outside class when you're not there.
3. Put an unsuccessful model or unsuccessful examples of the task on the board. Ask learners to discuss in groups what feedback they could give.
4. Elicit their ideas and discuss as a class. During the discussion, note useful feedback phrases on the board or in the chat box.
5. Set up the final task. Ensure that at least one person in each group monitors while the others speak.
6. Swap the roles and repeat.
7. Give final whole-class feedback on both the task achievement and the peer feedback.

Take it further

Success criteria won't always be as clear as the example above. Despite this, it is always important for learners to give each other constructive and supportive feedback. Hedging language helps to avoid speakers sounding too direct or forceful, for example when giving advice and feedback. Here are some examples of sentence prompts using hedging which you could teach:

- 'You could consider…'
- 'If you wanted, you could try…'
- 'You might want to…'
- 'It might sound even better if you…'
- 'Maybe next time, try…'

Setting up effective repetition

Tips

As discussed in **Part A, Key principle 5: Creating prime conditions for dialogic feedback**, repetition is hugely important when it comes to retention. Despite this, learners often say 'Teacher, we've done that already!' The teacher knows that completion of the task is not the end in itself. However, it is easy to see why learners might think it is if they haven't been told the aims and objective for the lesson or the task or been given the tools to measure their own success.

Imagine that learners in an intermediate (B1) group have learnt to tell transport nightmare stories using narrative tenses and a range of collocations for transport issues. At the end of the lesson, they stand up, find a partner and tell their stories. The teacher claps and they move to new partners and tell their stories again. They do this another two times before sitting down and receiving whole-class feedback from the teacher. How do you think the learners might feel in this situation?

They might feel bored, confused or frustrated as they have just completed the exact same task four times without seeing any progression. By the time they receive feedback, it is too late as the activity has finished, as has their opportunity to practise the language from the lesson. Setting up repetition that works relies on learners seeing that it is an effective use of their time and most importantly, that they are making progress.

Task

Consider the situation in Tips. How would you change this activity so that learners can see the benefit of repetition and notice their progress? Look at the **Answer Key** to check your ideas

Try it out

1. Before the final task, get learners to decide on their personal success criteria.
2. Carry out the task and give feedback however you have planned.
3. Explain that they are now going to repeat the task but with an extra layer of success. Use these questions to help learners decide what to focus on:
   a. What will you do better next time?
   b. Is there anything you want to add?
   c. Is there anything you want to change?
   d. Is there anything you want to take away?

Take it further

As learners get used to repeating activities and improving on them, you can begin to repeat activities across multiple lessons. Repeat the final activity from one lesson at the beginning of the next. Before the activity, give learners planning time with these guiding questions:

- What did you do well last time?
- What do you want to do better this time?
- What specific language or skills are you going to use to do this?

Making homework meaningful

Tips

One of the biggest challenges we face as teachers is bridging the gap between the classroom and the real world and encouraging our learners to actually practise what they have learnt in their lives outside the classroom. Learners, the institution, or other stakeholders such as parents might expect homework to be set. They might have expectations of what form that homework should take. For example, they might expect a worksheet with grammar or vocabulary exercises. However, while these kinds of exercises can be useful, they tend to consolidate a single aim in the lesson as opposed to the objective itself. If the lesson has had a speaking or writing objective, then the homework should consolidate or extend this objective in a way that will benefit learners in their real lives. Depending on the objective of the lesson, these homework tasks could include:

- Speaking with a classmate or English-speaking friend and recording the conversation (with their permission).
- Speaking with a classmate or English-speaking friend and reflecting on the conversation.
- Leaving a review or comment online.
- Writing a message to a classmate using school social media.
- Writing an email to a company requesting information.

As learners can have such clear expectations for homework, when first setting up activities that encourage them to practise the objective of the lesson in a meaningful way, it is important to dedicate some lesson time to setting these activities up effectively. When discussing the homework task with your learners, encourage them to consider:

- What feedback they received in the lesson that will help them to achieve this task.
- What language and skills from the lesson they want to focus on in this task.
- How they will achieve this task practically i.e. Will they record it on their phone? Will they speak with a classmate or a family member?

Task

1. Look at Lesson 2: Spoken film reviews, for pre-intermediate (A2/B1) level learners.
2. Write a homework task that allows learners to practise the objective of the lesson.
3. Write 2-4 discussion questions you would give your learners when you set the homework to help them prepare for this task.
4. Look at the **Answer Key** to check your ideas.

Try it out

For your next lesson, plan a homework task that will give your learners the opportunity to practise the objective of the lesson in a meaningful way. Ensure that there is enough time planned at the end of your lesson to discuss with learners what language and skills from the lesson they want to practise.

Take it further

It is important that learners can see how the lesson objective can be directly applied to their lives. Sometimes that link will be clear, but sometimes it might be less so. There are also often other applications for the language and skills in your lessons that might not be immediately apparent. Once your learners are used to having these discussions, you can extend them by asking them 'In what other situations could you use this language and these skills?'

If we take the Task example of spoken film reviews, the structure of spoken reviews could be applied to reviews of books, restaurants, school subjects, music, TV shows, etc. Much of the language in the Vocabulary focus section could be applied to reviews of TV shows or books, and the recommendations could be applied to virtually any event or activity.

Helping your learners to see how language can be used in different situations ensures that everyone in the lesson can apply it no matter their interest, broadening the applicability of your lesson to the learners and strengthening the bridge between the lesson and learners' lives beyond the classroom.

Setting up effective post-lesson repetition

Tips

Sometimes there simply will not be time to repeat an activity during a lesson. However, that does not mean that learners need to miss out on the opportunity to upgrade their attempts using the information they gleaned from the feedback and reflection stages. This repetition can occur outside class time. Depending on the task you're trying to repeat, some will be easier than others. For example, a writing task can be set as homework as learners can work individually. Similarly, single turn speaking tasks in which there is only one learner speaking (e.g. telling a story), the learner can carry this out individually. However, when it is a group task this becomes trickier. Whatever the task, the key to success comes from ensuring learners have the information they need to carry out the activity without your presence.

These are the success criteria for effective post-lesson repetition tasks. Learners must know:

- ☐ Who they should be working with.
- ☐ When they should be working with them.
- ☐ How they should contact each other.
- ☐ What the key steps for the task are.
- ☐ What success looks like for the task.
- ☐ What they are trying to improve upon.
- ☐ What they need to submit (e.g. written task / audio / etc.)
- ☐ When they need to submit it by.

Depending on your context, technology can play an important role in achieving success with post-lesson tasks. Most learners, outside of very young learners of course, will have phones with which audio can be recorded so learners can submit recordings of their task. Note: this relies on your school having the means for learners to submit homework files safely and securely.

Task

1. Read the instructions and success criteria for a task about discussing TV shows.
2. Use the success criteria in Tips to assess the instructions.
3. What would you add or change to make these instructions more effective?
4. Look at the **Answer Key** to check your ideas.

Instructions	Success Criteria
You are going to discuss TV shows you like/dislike with your partners. 1. Prepare a list of TV shows you like/dislike. 2. Contact your partners. 3. Record the conversation of you discussing your list with your partners. 4. Listen back to your conversation and use the success criteria to assess it. 5. Record it again if you are not satisfied. 6. Send your recording to the teacher for feedback.	**Successfully discussing TV shows with others means:** ☐ Sharing your opinion of the show using like/dislike phrases. ☐ Giving reasons for liking/disliking. ☐ Agreeing/disagreeing with each other politely. ☐ Giving recommendations using 'You should check it out.'

Try it out

1. In your next lesson, plan for the repetition which you would like to take place after the lesson.
2. Use the example and the success criteria in Tips to write your instructions.
3. If this is the first time you have carried out a task such as this outside class, dedicate appropriate time in the lesson to explaining the task. The more often you do these kinds of tasks, the less time you will need to spend on instructions.
4. In your next lesson spend some time giving feedback on the tasks.

Take it further

It is not always necessary for learners to carry out the exact same task as they did in class in order to improve on their attempts from the lesson. For example, if learners have carried out a conversation in pairs in class, they could repeat the activity in a text chat and submit a screenshot of the conversation for feedback.

Post-lesson outcome mining

Tips

We can never fully anticipate what learner needs will emerge as we teach a lesson. We can plan and predict, we can consider possible problems and solutions, but then a conversation will take a turn we had not considered as one of our learners shares something about their life. These tangents can be brief moments in which we quickly teach an item and move on, they can be tangents that we choose not to take as they would distract from our objective, or they can be unintended learning opportunities that actually build towards our objective and add to our lesson. There might be many such learning opportunities in a single lesson.

Task

Imagine you are teaching an intermediate (B1) group and your lesson aims and objective are:

We are learning to (WALT):
- Give a presentation about your city that is easy to follow.

What I'm looking for (WILF):
- A clear introduction.
- Clear signposting for each stage of the presentation.
- Stressing your signposting language and pausing briefly after it.
- A range of vocabulary related to cities and what is in them.

During your lesson, the following situations arise.
- **Situation 1:** During a lexis input stage about places and activities in a city, one of your learners asks you how to say their job title in English.
- **Situation 2:** During a skills stage focusing on using signposting to help your audience follow your presentation, two learners tell you that they have trouble understanding a man who works in the school café because he has an Irish accent.
- **Situation 3:** During a skills stage focussing on the importance of maintaining eye-contact with your audience, one of your learners explains that they are a public speaker in their language and have some tips on how to use body language to keep your audience's attention and help them to follow the talk.

What would you do in each situation? Keep the overall aims and objective in mind when you decide. Look at the **Answer Key** to check your ideas.

Try it out

1. Before the final task, ask learners to discuss what they learnt in the lesson today which was not included in the aims.
2. Create a mind map of all the language and skills that have come up throughout the lesson.
3. Ask learners to discuss which of them would be useful in the final production task.
4. When negotiating success criteria for the final task, encourage learners to include their chosen language from the outcome mining.

Take it further

Involve your learners in the choices of the lesson. As possible tangents arise, give them the following choices as a group (adapted to the level of your learners):

- Will this help us to achieve the lesson objective?
- Is this a quick answer that is worth exploring?
- Should we examine this in more detail in a future lesson?
- Should we set research into this for homework?

These questions avoid the binary question 'Should we answer this question or not?' They allow for an element of learner autonomy and choice in how the lesson is managed give clearer guidance to learners on the kind of decisions you make as a teacher in their lessons.

Chapter 5

Skills development

Introduction

When it comes to skills teaching, there are a number of options available to an English teacher. The first is an integrated skills lesson in which a number of skills are practised together. For example, learners might read a text and talk about the topic, or they might listen to a conversation and then write an email to one of the speakers. In these situations, learners are not necessarily developing their skills overtly, they are practising or being tested on them. There is an argument that practice makes perfect and doing listening will lead to competency in this skill. However, as we argued in **Part A, Key principle 5: Creating prime conditions for dialogic feedback**, informed repetition is what leads to development. This means setting up informed practice for learners, helping them to understand how and why they are doing this task. The tasks in this chapter will help you to discuss skills so that learners can develop them and apply them to their lives outside the classroom.

In this chapter, you will find the following tasks:

- **A successful skills development lesson:** How to plan a skills development lesson that drives the discussion and development of a particular sub-skill.
- **Talking about listening / Talking about reading:** How to discuss listening and reading sub-skills.
- **Discussing comprehension:** How to encourage the real-life discussion of comprehension.
- **Giving a written record of a skill:** How to help learners make notes about the sub-skills they have practised.

A successful skills development lesson

Tips

In a lesson in which the objective (or one of the objectives) is to develop a particular sub-skill (e.g. learning to read online news articles for gist), a section of the lesson should be given over to the overt discussion of this sub-skill. This is similar to how you might include overt discussion in a systems lesson, focussing on language areas such as grammar, vocabulary, pronunciation or discourse features.

First of all, let's consider the basic format of a successful systems lesson with a language focus. If the lesson was focusing on grammar, these might be the success criteria:

- ☐ The main input of the lesson focuses on the system (the grammar point) and how to use it (e.g. in a conversation).
- ☐ The learners leave the lesson with a written record about the grammar (written information about the grammar point which they could refer back to after the lesson).
- ☐ They would practise the grammar.
- ☐ There would be success criteria (focused on how to use the grammar in a real-life situation).
- ☐ They would receive feedback on how successfully they had used the grammar.
- ☐ They would reflect on/discuss how this grammar could be used outside the classroom.

In a successful skills development lesson, the only thing that changes is the focus, moving from a system to a sub-skill. This means we could say that the success criteria for an effective sub-skills development lesson are:

- ☐ The main input of the lesson focuses on the sub-skill and how to use it in a particular situation.
- ☐ The learners leave with a written record about the sub-skill (written information about the key features or strategies of the skill and its use).
- ☐ They would practise the sub-skill.
- ☐ There would be success criteria (focused on how to use the sub-skill in a real-life situation).
- ☐ They would receive feedback on how successfully they had used the sub-skill.
- ☐ They would reflect on / discuss how this sub-skill could be used outside the classroom.

Task

In this example lesson, a pre-intermediate (A2/B1) group are working towards this objective: 'By the end of the lesson, you will be better able to read an article for gist (e.g. to assess your interest and decide whether to read it in more detail)'. Here is a summary of the main lesson stages:

- Learners talk about the topic of the article.
- They read the article and answer gist comprehension questions.
- They check their answers to the gist questions.
- They learn vocabulary from the article related to the topic.
- They speak about the topic using the vocabulary.
- They receive feedback on their use of the vocabulary.

1. Evaluate this lesson. Does it meet all of the success criteria for a skills development lesson from Tips?
2. What could you add or change to increase its success?
3. Look at the **Answer Key** to check your ideas.

Try it out

1. Look back at a recent sub-skills development lesson you have taught.
2. Use the success criteria for a successful sub-skills development lesson from Tips to evaluate your lesson.
3. Write the steps you would take to approach this differently next time.

Take it further

In general, lessons will often end with feedback on how well learners have achieved the lesson objective or with a discussion on the topic of the lesson. When it comes to sub-skills development, one of the challenges a teacher faces, is helping learners to see how the skill they have learnt in the class can be applied to other contexts. Finish your next sub-skills lesson with the following questions:

- What skill did we develop today?
- In what other situations could you use this?
- How will you practise this before your next lesson?

The use of the word 'will' encourages learners to make a commitment to practise this skill. Speak to learners in the next lesson and discuss how they got on. By making it an ongoing conversation, learners will become used to talking about skills just like they would about grammar or vocabulary.

Talking about listening

Tips

In Richards and Renandya's anthology of current practice published in 2002, David Nunan refers to listening as a Cinderella skill, meaning it had been researched less than the other three skills, less had been written on it and there was less guidance for teachers on how to approach teaching it. While this has certainly changed since then and more and more is being written on listening, at the time of writing many coursebooks still focus on practising listening rather than developing it. One possible reason for this is that progress with listening skills is less tangible than spoken or written progress. Listening strategies are also generally more challenging to discuss than reading strategies, where there is more support for comprehension in common features of texts like headings, bullet points, topic sentences, etc. This has led to listening rarely being discussed in the language classroom. The Overt Teacher encourages the discussion of listening skills in their classroom, helping raise learners' awareness of their role in the listening process.

This does not however, mean that teachers need to carry out deep research into listening sub-skills and strategies before they can discuss it in their classrooms. When discussing listening, it is as simple as moving away from checking how many comprehension questions a learner got correct and instead talking about what they found challenging and why. We must dig deeper into what learners did and didn't understand, why and what can be done to help learners them improve. A simple way to encourage this discussion is to introduce questions before and after listening tasks. By doing this regularly both the teacher and learner become used to discussing the listening process. Here are a few examples of possible questions:

Before the task

- You're about to listen to [insert text type e.g ______]. What do you think you will find challenging?
- What strategies can you use to make it less challenging?

After the task

- Did you lose your place in the listening?
  What did you do when this happened? Did it help?
  What could you do differently next time?
- Which parts of the listening were challenging to understand?
  What strategies did you use to help you in this situation? Did they help?
  What strategies could you use next time?
- In what other situations could you use these strategies?

By having overt discussions like this little and often, over time learners will build up their strategies for listening, and their awareness of when they can be applied.

Task

In this pre-intermediate (A2/B1) lesson, learners listen to a radio interview about climate change. Before they listen, they learn some vocabulary on the topic. After listening, they complete a true/false comprehension task.

1. What discussion questions would you ask to help learners discuss the process of listening?
2. Which questions would you ask when?
3. What might you expect the learners to say in answer to your questions?
4. Look at the **Answer Key** to check your ideas.

Try it out

Learners may not be used to discussing listening strategies and they may struggle the first time you ask them to. After all, when asking a grammar question there is often a right or wrong answer. When it comes to discussing listening strategies, it is less about what is correct or incorrect and more about which strategy works for a particular individual. Ease the learners in with short, regular conversations.

1. After the next listening task you do, ask learners to discuss what strategies they used to help them understand the text. Note that at this point the learners may not have strategies. You could write some suggestions on the board and asking learners to decide which ones might help them in this situation.
2. Replay the listening and ask learners to apply the strategies they have chosen.
3. As a group reflect on how well their chosen strategies worked for them. Note that not every strategy will work for everyone in every situation, but avoiding the conversation means everyone remains uninformed.
4. Before the next listening task, ask learners to discuss in pairs what they think will be challenging about it. Discuss it as a group, encouraging learners to offer solutions to each other's expected challenges. Offer any suggestions of your own.

5. Help them to select strategies based on the ones discussed in the previous lesson/task.
6. Carry out the listening task.
7. Ask learners to reflect on how effective their chosen strategies were.

Take it further

One of the issues with listening skills is that it can be challenging to remember what issues happened during the listening, ready to discuss them after the listening task. In some lessons, you could follow these steps and have more immediate conversations.

1. Play the listening. Ask learners to raise their hand when they are lost or finding the listening challenging. Tell them that this is to help them to understand which parts of the listening are more challenging for them.
2. When learners raise their hand, stop the recording and discuss as a class what they found challenging, what they can do to help themselves, or what others are doing to overcome this challenge.

Talking about reading

Tips

It is quite common for English-language materials to include a reading text as part of the lesson which is mostly used as a vehicle for the grammar or vocabulary in the lesson, with examples from the texts used to show how that language can be used in context. Around these texts, reading sub-skills are often practised or tested, but they might not be discussed overtly, or developed such that learners can notice their progress with the sub-skill.

The following is an example of what a reading text and the associated tasks might include in published materials at the time of writing.

Jewellery Thieves Caught in the Act

Late last night police were called out to Boyle's Jewellery store on 7th Avenue to reports of a robbery. It was only when they arrived that they realised that it was the robbers themselves who had called for help.

The thieves had locked themselves in the store's vault and were afraid of running out of air before morning. Police arrested the two unlucky thieves, who will be sentenced tomorrow. The manager of Boyle's has refused to comment on the safety of their vaults.

Activity 1

a. Read the headline to the online article. What do you think this article is about?

b. Read the article quickly to check your ideas.

Activity 2

Read the article in more detail. Answer the questions with true (T) or false (F).

1. The owner of the store called the police.
2. The robbers were running out of the store when they were caught.
3. The manager of the store was happy to speak with the reporter.

What sub-skills are being practised here? In Activity 1a, learners predict the content of the article using the headline, practising the sub-skill of prediction based on features of a particular genre, in this case headlines in articles. In Activity 1b, learners practise the sub-skill of reading for gist. They are asked to read quickly rather than in detail. In Activity 2, learners are asked to read for detail and to answer comprehension questions.

The skills of predicting text content, reading for gist and reading for detail are often practised in materials but rarely actively discussed or developed. Perhaps the assumption is that practise makes perfect and that these skills are transferrable from a learners' L1. After all, this is how we might approach reading an article in any language: we use features of the genre to make predictions and decide if it is vaguely of interest; then we read it quickly to see if it is worth reading more carefully; then if we're interested, we read it in more detail and identify specific details that we might want to pass on to others.

However, is it enough to practise these sub-skills without drawing attention to them? Key principle 3 of the Overt Teacher is that a learner should be involved in discussions about what they are learning. It might be that our learners can carry out these sub-skills effectively in their L1. It might be that they can do so in English too, but without overt discussion with learners about what they do and how they do it, we cannot know this, and we cannot support those who need more help.

The success criteria for a successful discussion about a reading sub-skill are therefore that learners should:

- ☐ Know why the skill is important.
- ☐ Reflect on strategies they currently have for achieving this skill.
- ☐ Reflect on new strategies they learn during the lesson.
- ☐ Know how they will practise this skill in their life outside the class.

Task

1. Look at Activity 1b from the example in Tips.
2. Write 2-5 discussion questions you could set for a group of pre-intermediate (A2/B1) learners to raise their awareness of the features of this sub-skill.
3. Look at the **Answer Key** to check your ideas.

Try it out

1. Choose a reading task that practises a reading sub-skill.
2. Decide what sub-skill is being practised and write it in your own words.
3. Write down the strategies you would use yourself to achieve this sub-skill (e.g. reading the first and last lines of a paragraph to gist read a long text).
4. Write 2-5 questions that will help your learners to discuss this sub-skill and reflect on their own approaches.
5. Before learners carry out the task, give them the questions to discuss.
6. Discuss possible strategies and approaches as a whole class.
7. Let learners apply the strategies they discussed, then reflect on how useful they were.
8. The next time this skill arises, elicit strategies from learners again before proceeding with the task.

Take it further

Bridging the gap between the classroom and the real world can be a real challenge for teachers, especially when it comes to reading sub-skills. They can be seen as something that is practised in the classroom and tested with comprehension questions. After you've raised awareness of the features of a sub-skill and possible strategies in a lesson, give learners time to apply this skill to a real-world text using their phone. This could be a text you supply or something they would commonly read themselves. This has the dual benefit of practising the skill in a meaningful way and mirroring how learners often read on their devices outside the classroom.

Discussing comprehension

Tips

When bridging the gap between the classroom and the real world, one of the challenges is that many common classroom tasks do not obviously transfer into the real world. For example, it is highly unlikely that after reading an article outside the classroom, someone will ask me to answer true or false questions to check what I understood. While these kinds of activities are important tools for a teacher and allow them to easily check comprehension, they do not accurately mirror our learners' reading or listening experiences outside the classroom. The Overt Teacher promotes the discussion of comprehension through tasks which mirror the world outside the classroom.

If we consider the types of activities we do after reading, watching or listening to something outside the classroom, they often include:
- Summarising what we read / saw / heard.
- Discussing why we liked / didn't like it.
- Giving our opinions on the story, characters, writing, etc.
- Making recommendations and giving reasons for them.
- Relating the text to our own lives and experiences.
- Using information from the text to support our opinions or arguments.

Task

1. Read the short story in the box, taken from our book *Textploitation*.
2. Write 2-4 questions you could ask your learners that would both:
   a. reveal their comprehension.
   b. mirror the kind of discussion you might have after reading a short story outside the classroom.
3. Look at the **Answer Key** to check your ideas.

Life in the countryside

The wind burst through the trees, spraying the ground in sunlight. Barry stood breathing in the sunshine and wishing for the first time in his life that he had grown up in the country. It was an amazing feeling. Brenda came from the kitchen, stepping carefully on the soft ground in her heels. She wasn't quite used to the rural lifestyle... not yet...it would come...he hoped it would come anyway.

'Seriously, this ground is not what I'm used to. Honestly, Barry. I'm so fed up. You promised me the high life... *this* is definitely not it,' she said, looking around at the farm that he had moved her to. 'For once I just wish you would do what you say and say what you do, and I wish I didn't have to live on this awful farm!'

Barry knew she'd get used to it, but it wouldn't happen overnight. He was going to have to put up with her complaints for the next few months. Unfortunately, he wasn't sure he could anymore. He wasn't sure he could hold his tongue for much longer.

'You know what, Brenda? You know what I wish? I wish you could cook, I wish you could make it through a day without needing four naps. I wish you weren't dangerously underweight. I wish you would look at me with anything but hatred. But most of all...most of all...I wish you would just leave me alone from time to time,' he said without raising his voice or looking at her.

He left Brenda and her heels to sink into the mud and walked off to muck out the pig pen. Turns out he couldn't hold his tongue for much longer at all.

Try it out

1. Identify key reading and listening texts in your lesson materials.
2. Write one question for each text that will
   a. reveal learners' comprehension.
   b. mirror the kind of discussion you might have after reading or listening to this kind of text outside the classroom.
3. In class, use these discussion questions before or instead of traditional comprehension activities. Note that these discussions do not have to take long!
4. Repeat these activity types regularly and gradually build up your learners' summarising, opinion-giving, and recommending skills and language.
5. Discuss with learners how these skills and this language can be used outside the classroom.

Take it further

Whether it is a video, an online comment, an article or a story, we very often share our understanding and feedback through non-verbal or linguistic means. If you were to share a video online, commenters might leave a GIF, a meme, or string of emojis that reveals their opinion and interpretation of that video. In order to spark the conversation on comprehension, first ask your learners to share a GIF or meme (or whatever is currently popular and appropriate) with their partners and then to discuss why. The discussion which follows will inevitably reveal their understanding and interpretation of the text, while also mirroring their real lives.

Giving a written record of a skill

Tips

The Overt Teacher will discuss sub-skills and strategies with their learners, break them down into easily manageable stages and provide a written record that learners can return to at a later date for tips and strategies to help them apply that skill effectively in their lives outside the classroom.

In this example for an upper intermediate (B2) lesson, the objective is 'To be better able to understand a presentation, focussing on noticing signposting to understand the structure of the talk.' A possible written record of this sub-skill would be:

> Sometimes when listening to a presentation, we can get a bit lost. Most speakers will use words and phrases to help you to understand their talk or refocus your attention if you get lost or lose concentration. This is called 'signposting'.
>
> When listening to a presentation, remember:
> - Signpost words are usually stressed (spoken clearly).
> - The speaker will usually pause after the signpost.
> - Signposts will tell you the type of information coming next:
>   - *However, / While / Although* = followed by contrasting information
>   - *Importantly, / It's important to remember / Crucially* = followed by key points
>   - *Finally, / In conclusion,* = followed by final points
>
> You can use signposting to help you understand where you are when listening to a presentation, so listen carefully for it.

A successful written record of a sub-skill will:
- ☐ Be short.
- ☐ Be focused on a single sub-skill.
- ☐ Use language at or below the learners' level.
- ☐ Contain a task (e.g. a gapfill) to help the learner process the information more deeply.
- ☐ Include why it is an important sub-skill.
- ☐ Include when it can be applied.
- ☐ Include practical information, tips and strategies for applying the sub-skill.

Using these success criteria to evaluate our written record, we can see that:
- ☐ It is short and focused on one sub-skill. When the focus is too broad, it can be overwhelming for learners and harder for them to apply to their lives outside the classroom.
- ☐ The language included in the record is appropriate for the level. There is no new terminology and examples are given to help learners understand.
- ☐ It includes real-life examples of why this is an important sub-skill and when it can be applied (e.g. 'helping you refocus on presentations').
- ☐ There are practical tips that help learners (e.g. 'The speaker usually pauses after the signpost.')
- ☐ As there is there is no task associated with it, it will be harder for learners to process it deeply.

Task

1. The written record above has no activity associated with it to help learners process it more deeply. Remove some of the words to create a gapfill from it.
2. Look at the **Answer Key** to check your ideas.

Try it out

1. The next time you teach a sub-skill, prepare a written record of it before the lesson.
2. Check it against the success criteria in Tips.
3. Once you're happy with the content, remove some of the key words to turn the written record into a gapfill activity.
4. Teach your lesson as normal and after the input stage on the sub-skill, get your learners to complete the activity.
5. You can now use this record to:
   a. check their understanding of the sub-skill prior to any final practice stages.
   b. return to in future lessons when an opportunity to practice this sub-skill arises.
   c. help learners reflect following the final practice stage.

Take it further

Gapfills are useful tasks for written records because you can include the support of a box showing which words fill the gaps. This ensures learners are considering the gaps but not challenged too greatly, meaning the focus of discussions can remain firmly on the sub-skill which is being taught.

Another way to turn a written record into a task is to write True/False statements about the skill. We recommend that the majority of the answers are False in order to encourage discussions about why they are false and improve learners' understanding and retention of the sub-skill and related strategies.

C

Introduction

In this section we will explore how a more Overt Approach can be applied in a range of different situations, including different types of classes, different modes of delivery, writing materials, and working on your own professional development.

Throughout this book, we have mostly discussed group classes, learners who attend General English lessons as part of their mainstream education or those who have paid to study English either in-country or abroad. However, these are not the only learners who would benefit from a more Overt Approach to teaching. Whether a learner is studying General English, Business English, English for Academic Purposes (EAP), or English for Specific Purposes (ESP), the approach and techniques outlined throughout this book are applicable. This is what we discuss in Chapter 1.

The approach also remains the same whether learners are joining live online lessons, studying remotely via forum-based courses, studying in Virtual Reality (VR), or joining hybrid courses. This is what we look at in Chapter 2. We will examine how Overt Teaching can be applied to these contexts and modes of delivery as well as highlighting specific aspects particular to these contexts that would benefit from an Overt Approach.

In Chapter 3 we explore how to write materials which include the overt discussion of learning. This should help both teachers and learners to remember to make space for these discussions by including reminders in the materials.

Finally, in Chapter 4 we outline a step-by-step approach to overtly working on your own development as teacher. This shows how considering aims, objectives and success criteria is applicable beyond the classroom in other areas of our careers as teachers.

Each section includes a general discussion of how Overt Teaching could be useful in that situation and a specific example of how it could be applied.

Chapter 1

Overt Teaching in different contexts

Exam classes

Why is a more Overt Approach to exam classes needed?

There are many reasons a learner might take a high-stakes exam (such as IELTS, a Cambridge exam, or school-leaving exams) but often it is to take a life-changing step. This step might be moving to an English-speaking country or applying to a university that requires proof of the applicant's level of English as part of the application process. It might just be that having an official certificate proving their level of English will make that learner more employable. This means that exam classes are often more high pressure than general English classes. Another feature of exam courses is that there is usually time pressure. They tend to be finite and with a fixed end point, namely when the learners take their exam.

With such a clear reason for learning, we might take it for granted that learners would be clear on how what they are learning in class will help them in their future lives. However, in our experience, learners in exam courses tend to be focused on taking the exam, seeing it as the end point of their studies. Because of this preparing for an exam can encourage learners to only consider the short-term effects of their learning, rather than how it might help them in the future. This is where a more Overt Approach comes in, as it helps learners to look beyond the exam and consider the relevance of what their learning to their lives.

Connections between exams and real-life situations

At the time of writing, IELTS is the most common exam which learners take to prove their level of English to a UK university. The speaking section of this exam has three parts:

- **Part 1:** Test takers answer general questions about themselves and their lives.
- **Part 2:** Test takers are given a prompt and must speak for two minutes on the prompt. The prompt asks them to tell a story about their experience.
- **Part 3:** Test takers are asked more questions that encourage them to discuss the topic from part 2 but focusing on more abstract issues and possible solutions.

Now let's imagine you are a new student at university in an English-speaking country. You arrive and you attend an event to meet your new peers and classmates. When you first meet someone new, you'll probably tell them a little about yourself, where you come from and what your interests are. This is like Part 1 of the exam. As you get to know them, you may open up more and tell them stories about you, your life, and your experiences. Part 2 of the exam relates to this. As the event progresses, the major issues in the world might come up in conversation and you and your peers might discuss these abstract issues and suggest possible solutions. This is where Part 3 becomes relevant. In this simple example, we can see that the exam is testing how successful test-takers would be in this realistic future situation. In this way exam courses are preparing learners not just to pass an exam but to be successful in the next major step of their lives.

The same can be seen in the TOEFL speaking test in which test-takers must listen to common campus-based conversations and show their understanding of the conversation, a common situation in campus life.

The Overt Teacher helps their learners not just see how the skills and systems they are learning will be tested in the exam but also how they will benefit the learner in their life beyond the exam. The focus moves from the short-term goal of passing the exam to the long-term goal of preparing for the next steps in their lives. When learners can see the relevance of what they're learning and how it applies to their future lives, it can increase engagement and investment in the lessons.

Helping learners to relate exam tasks to their lives

Whatever the skill or system that is being developed, the Overt Teacher will help their learners see its relevance. How might one of these lessons look in practice?

Imagine that you are focussing on specific reading sub-skills from the exam. The Overt Teacher doesn't only discuss what specific skills are being tested and how these can be developed ready for the exam, but also how these sub-skills can be practised and employed in the real world. To do so, the Overt Teacher uses the following guiding questions when they are discussing a sub-skill:

1. Where in the exam is this sub-skill tested?
2. Do you have any strategies for this sub-skill? Do you need to ask your teacher or classmates for strategies?
3. Do you currently use this sub-skill outside the classroom?
4. When might you use this sub-skill in the future?

These questions help guide the discussion and if used frequently, they will mean that learners are aware of what they are learning and why, the first two key principles of Overt Teaching, as discussed in part A.

Let's take the reading tasks from the IELTS and TOEFL exams as an example. IELTS reading tasks often contain questions where a learner is asked to locate names or numbers in a text. Similarly, in TOEFL reading tasks, learners are often asked to identify a particular word or passage in a text. To do so effectively, learners will be required to quickly scan the text. If we ask learners questions 1-4 above, we might expect the following answers to emerge in the discussion:

1. The answer to this will depend on the exam you are preparing your learners for.
2. Possible strategies might be:
   a. Don't read each word individually.
   b. Know exactly what you're looking for and why you're looking for it.
   c. Only look for one word or phrase at a time.
   d. Let your eyes fall quickly down the page until you find the word or phrase you're looking for.
3. Every time I go to the train station and look for my train on the departures board, I have to use this sub-skill. / Every time I order a coffee and check the prices on the board. / Every time I look at a menu and try to find the vegetarian options.
4. At university, I will need to check texts for specific words to see whether it is relevant for me and I need to read more. If I read the whole text every time, I will waste a lot of my time.

Whatever the sub-skill, language point or lexical set, the key is to expand the discussion beyond the exam task and help learners to see why they are learning it and how important it will be in their futures. In our experience, these discussions improve engagement and aid retention as learners really see the value in what they're learning.

English for Academic Purposes (EAP)

Why is a more Overt Approach to EAP classes needed?

EAP courses often work towards ensuring learners are able to achieve what is required in assessments, meaning there can sometimes be a large gap between the learners' expectations of what might be included in a course to prepare them for success in their academic studies, and the teacher's or curriculum's goals. Scott and Tann (2021) suggest this is due to learners not understanding the relevance of elements of a class. De Chazal (2014) emphasises the value of building a partnership between a teacher and the learners to encourage them to take responsibility for their own learning, and the need for the teacher to facilitate an environment conducive to this. If we can use this as a starting point, then the need for an Overt Approach to EAP teaching becomes apparent. This approach has the benefit of both further motivating learners and also ensuring that they can clearly see that what is taught has a value beyond the immediate need of the assessment, the completion of a particular task, or the contents of a particular lesson.

Applying EAP skills beyond the course

As an example, let's look at an EAP lesson where the objective is 'To be able to write an essay using a range of different sources to support your arguments.' One of the challenges that learners face in an EAP context is moving from environments in which shorter texts are quite common to being expected to read longer articles and books and identify the key information within these texts to support their arguments. The Overt Teacher will spend time discussing both the skills that their learners will need to employ in this research process, and also why these skills are important and how they will benefit them after the course. In this activity from the lesson, learners how successful application of a range of sub-skills connected to examining different sources might benefit them.

Skill	How might this skill benefit you in the research process?
Scanning	
Skim reading	
Noting down references	

Possible answers might be:

Skill	How would this skill benefit you in the research process?
Scanning	Scanning will help us to look for key words in texts and in indexes. This helps us to identify if a book or article contains the information we require without needing to read the entire text.
Skim reading	Once we know that a text has some of the key words we're interested in, skim reading can help us to identify if the information is relevant for our essay. We can then decide whether to abandon the text or read it in detail. This can save us a lot of time.
Noting down references	Writing down full quotes and the full reference will help us later when we come to write our bibliography. Otherwise we might find there are quotes that we need, which we cannot find.

To be fully successfully in their academic study, it is not enough for learners to know how to successfully use each of these skills. They also need to understand when they are appropriate skills to draw on. It is this discussion that can make the lesson feel more relevant for the learner and motivate them to apply what they have learnt in class to their lives.

Young learners (YL)

What do we mean by young learners?

For the purposes of this section, we will take Nunan's (2011) approach of dividing young learners into two groups:

- **Younger learners:** those in pre-school and the first two years of school.
- **Older learners:** those who have completed the first two years of school and are 'well established at school and comfortable with school routines.'

When might an Overt Approach to learning be relevant in YL classes?

One of the key differences between these two groups as identified by Nunan is what they understand about the learning process. Older learners have an increasing awareness of this process, as well as of 'themselves as language learners' (ibid), and many of the ideas we have discussed in the book so far could be used with them, not just with adults. Much of the research carried out by Hattie and his collaborators which was described in Part A directly related to school-age children, meaning the older learners in Nunan's definition. But what about Nunan's 'younger learners'? To what extent can they actually engage in meaningful discussions around learning? And, would it benefit them to do so?

To answer this question, we will return to the key principles of an Overt Teacher as outlined in Part A:

1. An Overt Teacher believes learners should know **what they are learning**
2. An Overt Teacher believes learners should know **why they are learning it**, namely how the things they are learning can be applied to their lives outside the classroom.
3. An Overt Teacher believes that a learner should be **involved in discussions about what they are learning**.
4. An Overt Teacher believes learners will benefit from **choosing and discussing their own levels of success**.
5. An Overt Teacher believes that learners should be involved in **dialogic feedback about their success**.

Even from a very young age these beliefs still apply. By starting young, we can develop an awareness of learning that will help learners throughout their education. How, then, can we begin to develop these skills and ensure that younger learners know what they're learning, why they're learning it and how to comment on their success?

Helping young learners to think about the learning process

The table on the next page shows an example of a phonics activity for four to five-year-olds which demonstrates how this can be achieved at a level that younger learners can manage.

In stage A, the teacher gives a clear justification for the activity. Learners can see how their learning will help them: they will be able to read these words. In stage B, the teacher is modelling success for this activity by showing how these sounds are pronounced successfully. The practice in stage C allows learners to demonstrate their understanding of success and to communicate it to each other. They are encouraged to engage in dialogue regarding their own success. At this age, it is important to note that we cannot expect much in the way of discursive feedback between learners. In monolingual groups, learners could use their L1 to give each other feedback. In multilingual groups, we can feed them language chunks like 'Try again'. This cycle repeats in stages D and E, where learners are shown success again and then have the opportunity to practise and discuss their own success. In this lesson, learners are aware what they're learning, why they're learning it, and what success looks like. They can engage in a dialogue regarding success, even if it might be limited due to their age and language level. This meets the requirements of principles 1, 2, 3 and 5, even though the learners are very young.

Principle 4 of being an Overt Teacher outlines that learners should have the opportunity to choose their own level of success. In this activity elements of choice can be introduced by giving learners some agency over the number of words they try to read aloud and whether they pronounce the individual sounds in their head or try them out aloud before reading the whole word aloud. Encouraging them to move towards reading the sounds in their head helps learners to move onto silent reading, the next stage after sounding words out.

The principles of Overt Teaching remain the same regardless of the age of the learners, though the activities and expectations surrounding the discussion of learning may differ. The younger learners of today will become the older learners of tomorrow, so it's important that we are developing their awareness of the learning process so that when they are older, they can engage fully.

Stage	Activity
A	1) The teacher explains that the learners are going to learn to read some new words.
B	2) The teacher displays flashcards of each of the key sounds and pronounces the sounds. 3) Learners repeat after the teacher.
C	4) In pairs, learners display flashcards from Stage B for each other, and their partner pronounces the sounds. 5) Partners give thumbs up as feedback if the sound is correct, thumbs down if not. Learners can say if they don't feel the thumbs up/down is accurate.
D	6) The teacher displays 3-letter words containing the key sounds. 7) The teacher pronounces each sound. 8) The teacher reads the word. 9) The teacher selects learners to read the word as a model for the class and corrects where necessary.
E	10) In pairs, learners display the words from stage D to each other. 11) Their partners pronounce each sound and then read the word. 12) Partners give thumbs up as feedback if the word is correct, thumbs down if not. Learners are encouraged to discuss if they don't feel the thumbs up/down is accurate.
F	13) Teacher monitors throughout helping individual pairs with any difficulties.

English for the workplace

Why might a more Overt Approach be needed?

English for the workplace includes business English and English for specific contexts like nursing or finance. Skills covered in the lessons might be managing meetings, emailing for a variety of purposes, or using register effectively in the workplace. The challenge for the teacher is that while all the learners have a similar goal of successfully using English in their chosen profession, those professions could range from nurses to architects to office managers to graphic designers, all in the same group. The teacher must ensure that each of these learners has their needs met and sees the relevance of the lesson. It is important, therefore, that throughout the lesson the teacher and learners are engaged in overt discussion around the relevance of each of the skills and the key language and are given the opportunity to decide which items of the target language can be applied to their context.

There are a number of factors to consider when discussing relevance with learners:

- **Register:** Is this item of lexis appropriate in their professional context? For example, asking for '10ccs of morphine, stat' might be appropriate in a hospital setting but replacing 'stat' with 'ASAP' would be inappropriate. Similarly, asking for a 'document to be sent over, stat' in an office setting would sound odd.
- **Intelligibility of lexis:** Depending on a learner's context, some items of lexis may make them less intelligible. For example, colloquialisms from British English may not be understood if the learner is working in an international context in which the majority of employees have English as a second language.
- **Intelligibility (pronunciation):** In certain contexts the use of connected speech might make learners less intelligible if it is not commonly used in the company.

This overt discussion is a thread that must be woven through any lesson in this teaching context.

Overt discussions: lesson aims and objective

Here is an example of a lesson on giving feedback in the workplace:

Today we are going to:

- Discuss what 'good' feedback means to you.
- Learn to deliver feedback (Evidence – effect – evaluation: 'I saw [X]. This had [Y] effect, which was great because [Z].')
- Learn to ask for further information ('You mentioned X, could you tell me more? /'When you say X, what do you mean?' / 'Going back to …')
- Learn to set the next achievable step for the feedback recipient (e.g. What will you do next? / How will we evidence that? / What will the criteria for success be?)

So that you can:

- Give positive and negative feedback (e.g. in an evaluation / appraisal)

To ensure learner engagement in this English for the workplace lesson, the conversation around relevance and learner context must begin at the start of the lesson. Useful questions might be:

- Do you have to give formal appraisals?
- Do you ever give feedback to colleagues?
- Is there a company-wide process and structure for giving feedback?

The answers to these questions will allow the teacher to adapt the language they present throughout the lesson and will inform how the learners personalise and judge their own success based on their own professional needs. Without these overt discussions throughout the lesson, the teacher is left with a one-size-fits-all lesson which some learners may not engage with.

Chapter 2

Overt Teaching with different technology

English has long been taught online and using different forms of technology. However, in 2020, the English-teaching landscape changed significantly. With schools forced to close around the world due to the outbreak of Coronavirus, teachers and learners moved into online teaching on a scale we had never seen before. A surprising side-effect of this situation was that many learners who may not have previously considered learning English online now had direct experience of doing so successfully. While all of the activities in this book can be adapted for online teaching, there are a number of features of online teaching which are specific to it. In this chapter we will examine how Overt Teaching can be applied to three particular modes of delivery:

- **Synchronous online teaching:** When the teacher and the learners are present for an online lesson at the same time. At the time of writing, common platforms for this type of teaching include Zoom, Microsoft Teams, and Google Classroom.
- **Asynchronous online teaching:** Input or practice that occurs in the learners' own time, without real-time support from the teacher. This could be forum-based tasks, exercises from a website, or whole courses such as those created on platforms like Moodle. Some courses combine synchronous and asynchronous teaching, described as **blended teaching**.
- **Virtual reality (VR) lessons:** Lessons carried out in a virtual reality environment in which the learners are completely immersed in the lesson through the use of technology such as VR goggles. Learners may or not be in the same physical space as the teacher and each other when participating in these lessons.
- **Hybrid lessons:** This generally refers to a group of both online and face-to-face learners studying simultaneously together.

Synchronous online teaching

Why might a more Overt Approach be needed?

Sending learners to complete tasks in breakout rooms can be an opportunity to create more independent learners who are able to carry out activities, self-assess, give peer feedback and employ the skills they will need in their lives outside the classroom. During these tasks, learners are mostly working without the direct support of their teacher, who has to divide their attention between all of the breakout rooms. While they spend time with one group, all other groups are effectively invisible to them. This is in contrast to a physical classroom, where the teacher can monitor all groups simultaneously and ensure they are on task. They can assess if a group needs further support by observing from across the room, without needing to be right next to them. Learners can put their hands up to get the teachers' attention if they need help. On many online platforms, alerts can be sent to summon the teacher, similar to putting up a hand in the physical classroom, but if learners believe incorrectly that they are completing the task correctly and effectively, they are unlikely to summon their teacher.

To successfully work independently on a task, learners must:

- ☐ Know the key stages of the task.
- ☐ Know what success looks like.
- ☐ Know exactly what their role is.
- ☐ Know what role the teacher will play in the task.
- ☐ Be able to self-assess / peer-assess the success of the task.
- ☐ Be able to give peer feedback on the success of the task.

An Overt Approach can be useful to help learners to develop these skills, increasing their ability to work autonomously and understand when they might need to ask the teacher for extra support.

A more Overt Approach to managing breakout rooms

In this example, learners complete a task in their online lesson in which they tell each other about their plans for the summer. There are three groups working in breakout rooms. Before they move to breakout rooms, the teacher provides them with the steps for the task and the target language in the chat box:

However, once in the breakout rooms, each of the groups approaches the task slightly differently:

- **Group 1:** The learners begin by chatting about what they did the previous weekend. One of the learners reminds them they are supposed to talk about their summer plans. They discuss their plans. One of them mentions they are going to the UK in July and they begin to talk about passport queues in Britain.
- **Group 2:** The learners cannot remember what their task is so they wait until the teacher arrives in the breakout room to monitor them. The teacher reminds them of their task and they carry it out step by step.
- **Group 3:** The learners begin by asking each other about their plans and discussing them. One of the learners remembers the list of target language and shares it in the chat box for the others. They discuss how well they did. They finish with some extra time left. One of the learners checks the task steps and reminds the others they have time to repeat the activity. They do so.

In each of these scenarios, the learners completed the task, and the teacher perhaps gave them feedback on the use of the target language which they noticed while they moved around the breakout rooms.

However, there is an extra layer here for the Overt Teacher to uncover and discuss. Through their monitoring, the teacher was aware of some of what learners were doing in the breakout rooms but only the learners know exactly what happened. Setting the following task reflection questions would help the teacher support learners in becoming more autonomous in future tasks:

1. Did you spend all of your time on the task?
2. How did you make sure you completed the task fully?
3. Is there anything you would do differently next time you're in a breakout room?

Following this discussion, with the teacher's help these learners might come to the following conclusions:

- **Group 1:** They could use the task steps in the chat box to keep them on task and give them time to upgrade their language by repeating the task (step 6). They should be wary of getting distracted by chatting about other topics.
- **Group 2:** They could have wasted less time by checking the task steps in the chat bow, or messaging the teacher if they were unable to find the steps.
- **Group 3:** What this group did could be used as an example to the other groups of how to manage when you are unsure of what to do next in a task.

Asynchronous and blended online teaching

Why might a more Overt Approach be needed?

Examples of asynchronous tasks include reading exercises, completing controlled practice activities, working on a project as part of a group, practising language from the lesson in a forum task, or reading and leaving comments on classmates' work, among others. Some courses will blend both synchronous and asynchronous learning, so it is possible to spend time in synchronous lessons discussing asynchronous tasks and how they will be completed. However, many online courses will be entirely asynchronous, with learners never spending any time teaching or learning simultaneously with classmates or teachers.

Much like with breakout rooms in synchronous online lessons, the success of asynchronous teaching relies on learners knowing what is expected of them without having a teacher there to get them back on track. Whatever the task, without the immediate support of the teacher, learners must find both the motivation to complete it and the time to do so, despite busy lives and distractions. The key to success is to remove as many obstacles as possible from the completion of the task. These obstacles could include:

- Not knowing exactly what the task entails.
- Not knowing why the task is important for them.
- Not knowing how the task will be assessed.
- Needing to contact a classmate to complete the task.
- Needing to access another system to upload or complete the task.

Removing obstacles requires careful planning of the task and overt discussion. Where possible, some tasks within the course, whether synchronous or asynchronous, should be dedicated to this discussion so that learners know exactly what is expected of them, who they need to work with, when they should do what and how they should communicate. Clear lines of communication are key,and it is crucial that tasks have instructions detailing exactly what the tutor's expectations are.

One specific example of this is when learners are encouraged, or even required, to leave feedback on the coursework submissions of their peers. Setting up a culture of peer feedback can help learners to feel part of a community of learners, rather than feeling isolated. Another benefit of establishing this community is that learners are developing their feedback and assessment skills, both valuable tools to any learner but especially the distance learner who will not receive regular on-the-spot feedback in lessons. As part of the overt discussion of instructions and expectations, it is important for tutors to communicate their expectations of peer feedback and how it will benefit the learners. This ensures learners are leaving effective feedback that the recipient can benefit from as well as developing their own assessment skills, as opposed to leaving vague or content-related feedback like the examples given in ⏩ **Part B, Chapter 4**, 'Setting up effective peer-to-peer feedback'.

Providing more overt guidance in forum tasks

In Version 1 of this forum task, learners are expected to leave feedback on the work of other members of their study group:

Version 1

1. Read the essay below on whether or not uniforms should be mandatory in primary schools.
2. Summarise the writer's argument and give your own opinion.
3. Leave feedback on the summaries and opinions submitted by other members of your study group.

However, without clear guidance and a fuller understanding of what is expected of them, learners are likely to be unsure of the type of feedback they should leave. An added awkwardness to leaving feedback comes from the fact that they may not have ever met their peers and might never do so. In the reworded example below, these barriers are removed.

Version 2

1. Read the essay below on whether or not uniforms should be mandatory in primary schools.
2. Summarise the writer's argument and give your own opinion. A successful summary should:
   - ☐ Be organised into 3 parts: an introduction, a summary of arguments, your opinion.
   - ☐ Identify the key arguments of the writer and briefly outline the supporting information.
   - ☐ Be easy for a reader to follow (because of the use of linking phrases).
   - ☐ Be written in a formal register.
3. Leave feedback on a minimum of 2 submissions from other members of your study group. Your feedback should:
   - ☐ Reference the criteria for success above.
   - ☐ Highlight areas of strength and give clear reasons about why these are strengths.
   - ☐ Be constructive, giving clear guidance on how a particular criteria could be improved.

In Version 2 of the task, the learners are given clear guidance, not only on how to achieve success in their own writing task but also on how to give effective feedback that they (and their peers) will benefit from. The success criteria for the summary work as both guidance for summary-writing and a reference point for feedback.

Course organisers could further increase the chances of success by adding examples of effective and ineffective feedback like those in the box below, as well as a reminder of the reason behind the task.

Examples

Use the examples below to guide you when writing your feedback. Remember, being able to assess the success of a piece of work, and give effective, objective feedback is a valuable learning skill that will help you to assess your own work. Please give your feedback some time and thought to benefit both you and other group members.

Ineffective feedback	Effective feedback
I really liked your summary. It was very good. I don't agree with your opinion though. I agree with the writer because I had to wear a uniform and I never had to think about what clothes to wear every morning.	Your summary highlighted all of the key arguments and supporting evidence. It was an effective summary as I was fully informed by the end of it. However, sometimes your register was a little informal. For example you used contractions and in your conclusion you wrote 'I feel like…'. Maybe 'It is my opinion that…' would be better.
This feedback does not give clear examples of strengths or guidance using the success criteria, which is the focus of the task. Instead, it focuses on the writer's opinions.	This feedback tells the summary writer clearly what they have done well and why. They also know what they need to improve and have a clear example of how to do so. The success criteria are referenced, and the feedback focuses on their ability to write a summary, rather than their opinions about the task.

Virtual Reality (VR) lessons

Why might a more Overt Approach to VR lessons be needed?

Virtual Reality lessons take place in fully immersive spaces. For example, learners could visit a virtual reality restaurant to practise ordering food. One of the key aspects of learning in VR is this total immersion in the virtual environment, which has the benefit of blocking out any outside distractors like phones. However, it also means that in the VR platforms available at the time of writing, learners do not have access to notes, note-taking facilities or materials like coursebooks or worksheets. Short messages can be sent to virtual watches or tablets, but in general, learners cannot rely on notes or coursebook materials. They must use the language they already have at their disposal, and it is the teacher's role to help them to activate and build on this language while they are in the VR space. In this way, the VR teacher often has to adopt a reactive role, giving feedback throughout the lesson and helping learners to reformulate and upgrade what they produce. Taking an Overt Approach helps the teacher to provide this feedback, and helps the learners see how it will help them meet the success criteria.

In VR, users are often represented by customisable avatars of themselves or stock avatars within the platform. At this early stage in the development of VR learning, research has already suggested that learning behind an avatar can 'benefit language learning by increasing immersion, engagement, and presence, and by reducing negative emotions like anxiety that impede language learning' (Thrasher, 2022, p5). This means that learners tend to be less inhibited in VR and engagement levels are often high. However, in a fully immersive VR environment where learners are able to stand up, walk around, pick up and virtually consume drinks and food, it can be easy to see how the focus could move to chatting or just playing.

Keeping the focus firmly on the task and the discussion of learning and progress means that:

- Learners are aware of the aim of the task.
- Learners can see how it will benefit them.
- Learners know what language and skills are required to be successful in the task.
- Learners know what role the teacher will play in the task (for example, will they be monitoring and feeding in necessary language or will they be taking part as the waiter?)
- Learners know what feedback will be given and when.

As discussed throughout this book, ensuring learners are aware of these points means involving them in overt discussion throughout the lesson.

How overt discussion can make a difference

Let's examine two lessons David observed in VR, with different groups of learners but with the same teacher, the same level (pre-intermediate, A2/B1), and the same lesson aims and objective:

Today we are going to:

- Learn cooking vocabulary.
- Discuss questions related to food(s) from our countries.
- Learn and practise common dialogues for ordering food.
- Reflect and receive feedback.

So that you can:

- Order a meal (e.g. in a restaurant / café).

With the first group, the teacher began the lesson in the VR classroom where learners were able to sit around a boardroom-style table. At the top of the virtual room was a whiteboard where the teacher displayed the aims and objective for the lesson. At the click of a button, the teacher teleported the group of learners to a virtual restaurant kitchen where there were shelves of ingredients, an open fridge full of ingredients, and a counter full of prepared meals, such as burgers, salads and pizzas. The teacher sent the learners off in groups to see what they could find in the kitchen. The learners soon realised that they could eat all of the ingredients (virtually of course), pick them up, throw them, and pour drinks and drink them. The teacher gave the learners five minutes to explore and then gathered them back together.

This is quite a common scenario in VR. It is a world without consequences in many ways so while learners are very engaged and perhaps even more willing than normal to engage in roleplay due to the use of avatars, their focus can often drift from the aims and objective of the lesson.

Following feedback with the teacher, David observed them again. They taught the same lesson to a different group of learners at a later date, but with very different results.

At the beginning of the lesson, the teacher spent time discussing the aims and objective with the learners and finding out what they already knew. Before they reached the kitchen, the teacher set up groups and explained the task to the learners, giving them clear task aims which fed into the lesson objective: 'You will have five minutes to find as many different meals and ingredients as possible. While you're walking around, I want you to discuss which ones you like and don't like. When we order food in the restaurant later on, you will be able to use the language we learn in the kitchen.' The teacher elicited some language for expressing likes and dislikes and sent it to the learners' watches so they could refer to it throughout. When they arrived in the kitchen, the teacher elicited the task aims again before sending them off to complete the task. Inevitably, learners began to play with the ingredients, but the teacher gently nudged them back on task by reminding them of the aims and objective.

While engagement was high in both lessons, in the second observation learners were able to use the target language much more successfully than in the first, where they tended to only rely on the safe language they had arrived in the lesson with. By taking a more Overt Approach in the second lesson, the teacher was able to help learners to stay focussed and move towards the lesson objective.

Hybrid lessons

Why might a more Overt Approach be needed in hybrid lessons?

In a hybrid classroom, there might be webcams set up in the classroom so that remote learners can see the face-to-face learners. With the help of a monitor or interactive whiteboard, those in class can see the remote learners. The teacher might make use of laptops or devices in the classroom to set up pairwork between learners from both groups. There are other ways to set up hybrid classrooms: in 2021, International House Manchester tried a hybrid learning environment with remote learners joining through virtual reality (Glew-O'Leary and Pepper). A big challenge for the teacher in any of these situations is ensuring that no learner is disadvantaged because of their mode of study or because there are two disparate groups within the same class, some studying online and some face-to-face.

Another challenge for the teacher is that their focus will inevitably be split and at any one time, they cannot be expected to give equal focus to both remote and in-person learners. How, then, can we achieve success in such an environment? Through careful planning and the overt discussion of roles and task aims, the hybrid teacher can make use of the in-person learners as facilitators. In her plenary talk at IATEFL British Council World Teachers' Day web conference 2020, Sophia Mavridi mentioned that this hybrid model would not 'work in a teacher-centred classroom' because the in-person learners 'take on very important roles and become assistants, and facilitators of learning'. An in-person learner can join the remote learners in a group and answer their questions or refer to the teacher if necessary; they can reply to questions from and in the chat box throughout the lesson; or they can give instructions to these remote groups. Without the overt discussion of task, task aims and roles, success in this scenario would be unlikely.

Success criteria and reflection

When setting up success criteria for tasks in a hybrid classroom, it is important that they reflect the scenario. Imagine a hybrid lesson in which there are six in-person learners and two remote learners who have joined the lesson online. There is a camera set up so that the remote learners can see the teacher and the whiteboard. There is a laptop set up on one side of the room so that in-person learners can be grouped with the remote learners. The objective of the lesson is 'To be better able to give advice (e.g. for relationship issues)'. Learners have been given a relationship problem and have to offer solutions. One of the in-person learners is grouped with the remote learners. Here are the success criteria which the teachers and the learners have agreed on:

Successfully giving advice for relationship issues means:

- ☐ Responding sympathetically to the issue.
- ☐ Giving advice using:
  - ☐ 'You should...'
  - ☐ 'If I were you, ...'
  - ☐ 'Why don't you...?'
- ☐ Using fast speech when giving advice.

To ensure that all learners are included and involved the teacher may choose to add criteria specific to the hybrid classroom. For example:

- ☐ Both online and in-person learners give advice.

This could also be included in reflection questions for the learners:

1. Did you respond sympathetically to the issue? How did you do so?
2. Did you give advice? What language did you use to do so?
3. Did everyone in the group offer solutions to the problem?
4. What would you do differently next time?

The hybrid teacher can use post-lesson self-reflection questions to monitor the engagement and involvement of both sets of learners:

1. Did all learners, both remote and in-person, take part in every task?
2. Was everybody aware of their role in the task?
3. Did all learners receive the same level of feedback?
4. Was everybody (whether remote or in-person) addressed in whole-class activities?
5. Were there any points where in-person learners were waiting for remote learners or vice-versa?
6. Is there anything I would do differently next time?

Chapter 3

An Overt Approach to creating teaching materials

Why Overt Teaching is rarely given space on the page

In Part A, we discussed the possible origins of what we defined as a Covert Approach to teaching. We partly attributed this to the materials which teachers use. We feel that what teachers see in the materials they are exposed to informs their choices in lessons and in the materials they create themselves.

Materials writers and editors must constantly make decisions about what to include on the page. The challenge is that there is a limited amount of space and a lot which they might need to include. Striking the balance between including all of the tasks and information necessary for completing the lesson objective, including images to create an interesting design, but also avoiding too much clutter the page can be a struggle. We are starting to see some overt discussions of learning in materials, but at the time of writing it is still quite unusual.

Consider a lesson with the following aims and objective:

Today we are going to:
- Watch an unsuccessful model of a presentation.
- Learn to organise a presentation.
- Learn to help your audience follow your presentation by:
  - Using signposting language.
  - Stressing (speaking clearly) signposting language.
  - Pausing after signposting language.

So that you can:
- Give a presentation that is easy for an audience to follow.

We can divide the key stages in this lesson into two categories:

1. Those that include input and practice.
2. Those that encourage the discussion of learning throughout the lesson, or Overt Teaching.

Stage	Lesson activity	Category
1	Discuss the aims and objectives of the lesson.	Overt Teaching
2	Watch an unsuccessful model of a presentation.	Input and practice
3	Discuss why it was unsuccessful.	Input and practice
4	Learn to organise a presentation.	Input and practice
5	Learn signposting language.	Input and practice
6	Learn to stress signposting language and pause afterwards.	Input and practice
7	Create success criteria for the presentations.	Overt Teaching
8	Prepare presentations in groups.	Input and practice
9	Deliver presentations.	Input and practice
10	Receive feedback from classmates using success criteria.	Overt Teaching
11	Reflect on success and consider what to improve next time.	Overt Teaching
12	Receive feedback from teacher based on success criteria.	Overt Teaching
13	Reflect on what's been learnt and how it could be used outside the class.	Overt Teaching

Without the input and practice stages, there is very little chance of success in this lesson so it can be easy to see why materials writers include these activities on the page. The problem is that without including any Overt Teaching activities on the page, they might be missed out by teachers, and learners might not understand why they are necessary. On the other hand, including all of them might be overwhelming.

When writing your own materials, it is therefore important to strike a balance between input and practice and Overt Teaching activities. By taking a little and often approach and including one or two of these activities in every piece of material you create, Overt Teaching activities can be given the importance they deserve, gradually becoming second nature for you as a teacher and for your learners.

See ⏩ **Lesson 3: Talking about your plans** for an example of a worksheet that includes overt discussions on the page.

For those readers who are keen to write their own materials or to include these discussions in their materials, what follows are some tips and ideas for managing their inclusion.

Three ways to take a more Overt Approach in your materials

1. The discussion of aims and objectives

Lesson aims are often included in a banner at the beginning of a coursebook unit or section. However, we rarely see both aims and a lesson objective included on the page. Displaying both the aims and objective on the materials allows learners to return to them easily throughout the lesson and to make notes on them to personalise them.

Most lessons begin with discussion questions to engage learners in the topic and find out what they already know and believe about it. The first of these questions could relate to the lesson aims, placing importance on the overt discussion of aims.

2. Success criteria

Success criteria for writing tasks are increasingly included in published materials. However, they could also be included for speaking tasks. If success criteria are included across a series of materials, learners will gradually learn to both use them and create them themselves. Below are three ideas for including success criteria in published materials.

Idea 1: Success criteria can be listed with tick boxes, giving learners the opportunity to reflect on their levels of success after an activity by ticking off what they feel they achieved.

Activity 1: Tell your partner about your plans for the summer. Remember to use the language and skills from the lesson.

Activity 2: Use these criteria to discuss how successful your conversation was:

A successful conversation about summer plans:

- ☐ Begins with a present continuous question.
- ☐ Uses the present continuous to discuss fixed plans.
- ☐ Uses 'might' to discuss possible plans.
- ☐ Shows interested by responding to plans.

Idea 2: Success criteria could be used prior to an activity for learners to choose which criteria they will focus on in the upcoming task.

You're going to tell your partners about your plans for the summer. Which of these criteria are you going to focus on in your first conversation?

A successful conversation about summer plans:
- ☐ Begins with a present continuous question.
- ☐ Uses the present continuous to discuss fixed plans.
- ☐ Uses "might" to discuss possible plans.
- ☐ Shows interested by responding to plans.

Idea 3: Across a series of materials, success criteria can gradually take up less space on the page as learners develop the skill of creating criteria themselves.

Activity 1: Before you tell your partner about your plans for the summer, write your success criteria.

A successful conversation about summer plans:
- ☐
- ☐
- ☐

Activity 2: Tell your partner about your plans for the summer.

3. Reflection and repetition

Many published materials end in a single communicative task that brings together the various linguistic elements of the lesson. The implicit signal behind this task is that this is the end of the lesson. However, for learners to be able to see their progress and take advantage of the benefits of an overt discussion of success, they need the opportunity to reflect and repeat the task. This can be easily built into the instructions of the final task. Here is an example:

Activity 1: You're going to tell your partners about your plans for the summer. Tick the criteria below that you're going to focus on in your first conversation.

A successful conversation about summer plans:
- ☐ Begins with a present continuous question.
- ☐ Uses the present continuous to discuss fixed plans.
- ☐ Uses "might" to discuss possible plans.
- ☐ Shows interested by responding to plans.

Activity 2: Discuss the questions below with your partner:

a. How well did you achieve your chosen success criteria?
b. What will you do differently in your next conversation?

Activity 3: Work with someone new. Tell them about your plans for the summer.

In this example, learners are instructed to carry out their task in Activity 1, using success criteria to prepare their answers. However, instead of the lesson ending there, Activity 2 gives them the opportunity to reflect on how well they have achieved the task and make a plan to upgrade their answer. Activity 3 asks them to try again with a new partner. Giving this reflection and repetition the importance of space on the page makes it more likely to take place in the lesson and more likely that learners are willing to engage in repeating the task.

Chapter 4

Overtly working on your own development

Why might a more Overt Approach to professional development be needed?

As mentioned in **Part A**, the aim of this book is not to tell teachers how to teach English but rather to create a basic lesson framework that enables the overt discussion of learning, a framework which can be applied to any teaching approach. This same framework can be applied to virtually any learning, including teacher development. We have to admit that sometimes this is still challenging for us to do ourselves though! Over the years, we have often found ourselves in the position where we are following various threads of professional development but if we are honest, we sometimes do it in quite a disengaged manner. These threads lie at the back of our mind as something we know we want and need to work on, but we rarely do it in any overt or meaningful way.

For example, for many years David was aware that while his learners were progressing through the levels at his school, their listening scores in their level tests did not show the same progression between mid-course tests and end-of-course tests as in other areas. He identified listening skills as an area of developmental need and any time a workshop on listening skills was put on, he would attend. However, it wasn't until he was doing a diploma-level course and listening skills were a key component that he actually developed in this area or took any real overt action. Have you ever found yourself in a similar situation?

Identifying an area of development was an important step for David but the goal of 'Learning to teach listening skills' was too wide-ranging and overwhelming for him. Instead, David would have benefitted from the following four steps:

1. Have overt discussion with learners.
2. Set developmental aims and objectives.
3. Establish what success looks like.
4. Engage in reflection and ongoing discussion.

We will now look at each of these steps in turn, using David's goal as an example to show you how you might use them for your own professional development.

Four steps to Overt Professional Development

Step 1: Have overt discussion with learners

Once an area of development has been identified, it is important to gather as much information as possible from your learners. Our experience has been that learners are open to their teachers trying to develop and wanting to try out new methods and approaches. It is in their interest after all.

By carrying out diagnostic listening exercises and discussing with his learners what they found challenging, David could have uncovered specific learner needs within listening that would have narrowed his focus. When David finally did carry out overt discussions with his learners, he discovered that one of the areas they were really struggling with was decoding connected speech. This gave him a clearer goal to focus on in his own professional development.

Step 2: Set developmental aims and objectives

Just like with a lesson, your professional development objective is what you want to achieve and your aims are how you will do this. In the same way as when planning a lesson, it is important to begin with what you want to achieve in your professional development and work backwards to identify the objective and aims. In this situation, David wanted to be better able to teach his learners to decode connected speech by the end of the term. Once that objective was established, he had a focus for the term and could work backwards and decide what actions he could take to achieve this. His aims and objectives became:

This term, I will:

- Ask my manager to identify a colleague who is effective at teaching learners to decode connected speech.
- Observe this teacher and make note of the techniques they use related to connected speech.
- Try out these techniques in my classes.
- Discuss with my learners which techniques they found effective.
- Request an observation from my manager with a focus on my teaching of connected speech.

So that I can:

- Better prepare my learners to decode connected speech in conversation.

Step 3: Establish what success looks like

Identifying a series of actions that you can take sets you on the right path, but it is also important to establish what success will look like so that you know when you get there. It might seem like it makes sense for David to set success as 'My learners are able to decode connected speech'. This might even have been a future indication of success for him but for the term in question, David was focusing on gathering ways to teach learners, trying these methods out and gathering feedback on his performance from his learners and his peers. In a way, David was the focus of this professional development objective, as opposed to his learners. Setting achievable success criteria ensures the focus is clear and measurable. For David, his success criteria were:

Being better able to prepare my learners to decode connected speech in conversations means:

- ☐ Knowing at least 5 activities / techniques I can use to teach my learners to decode connected speech.
- ☐ Getting positive feedback from my learners on these techniques.
- ☐ Using these techniques successfully in an observed lesson.

Step 4: Engage in reflection and ongoing discussion

Reflection on your teaching does not have to be a time-consuming exercise and there are many approaches. For some, reflection on the success of the day's teaching will be an inner monologue on the teacher's drive or cycle home, as Mario Rinvolucri describes in his September 2019 episode on the TEFL Training Institute podcast. For others, it might be more structured, with notes being made in a reflection diary or on lesson plans. For David it tended to be the former, spending his commute home thinking back on the tasks and techniques he'd tried out that day, going over his learners' feedback and deciding what to try out next.

Instead of individual reflection like David's, some teachers might prefer to have ongoing conversations instead. These conversations could be with an academic manager or a colleague. In the same podcast episode, Mario Rinvolucri suggested mutual supervision where colleagues meet at regular interviews and talk through what has happened in their class that week. The idea is that the listener avoids giving their own opinion or advice on what they are hearing. Instead, they are giving the opportunity for the speaker to 'share the inner monologue', the same one she would have 'as she drives home or cycles home.' To be most effective, these reflective conversations should be sustainable, regular and actionable. They are, by their very nature, overt discussions of learning and progress.

Whatever method you choose, successful reflection should be:

- **Overt**: You cannot wait for it to happen. You have to make a conscious decision to carry it out, particularly when you first start reflecting on your teaching. As it becomes a sustained habit, it is easier to maintain. David had to remind himself to think about his goals each time he left work.
- **Sustainable**: Be realistic when deciding how you want to reflect. Consider how and when it can fit into your daily life without too much extra time needing to be set aside, for example during your commute as David did.

- **Regular**: Reflection does not have to be every day, but it does need to happen regularly for you and your learners to benefit from it.
- **Actionable**: As you reach the end of your reflection, come up with an actionable step. Whether you were successful in your efforts or not, what one thing will you do next to continue developing? For David, he next looked at testing his learners' abilities to decode connected speech, moving on from developing his teaching techniques.

Following these four steps should help you to put yourself at the centre of your own professional development.

Lesson plans for Part B

There are three lesson plans in this section:

- **Lesson 1:** Talking about friends – intermediate (B1) level
- **Lesson 2:** Spoken film reviews – pre-intermediate (A2/B1) level
- **Lesson 3:** Talking about your plans - pre-intermediate (A2/B1 level)

Lessons 1 and 2 are used for some of the tasks in **Part B**. Lesson 3 accompanies **Part C, Chapter 3: An Overt Approach to creating materials**.

Note that you can find the lesson aims and objective for Lesson 1 in **Part B, Chapter 2, 'Beginning the learning conversation'**.

Lesson 1: Talking about friends – intermediate (B1) level

A. Introduction

Work in pairs. Discuss the questions.

1. Who is your best friend? How did you meet them?
2. Do you have close friends at work / school?

B. Learn by reading

Read three comments about different people. Who would you like to meet most? Why?

It's great that you're coming out for drinks tomorrow. Bindu is going to be there. I think you'll really like her. She started a few weeks ago and they gave her the desk next to mine. We got on[1] immediately. I think you guys will really hit it off[2]. She's hilarious.

I've been friends with Jay since college. He grabbed me on the first day and invited me to tea. We've been best friends ever since[3]. You're going to love him. He's quiet but really nice and he loves chatting about politics. I think you'll really get on with him.

My girlfriend is coming for drinks tomorrow. We've been together[4] for about four years. She's lovely. I think you'll have a lot in common[5]. She's really into[6] hiking and camping and things like that. You'll have loads to chat about.

C. Focus on vocabulary

Match the underlined words and phrases from the comments in Activity B (1-6) to their meanings (a-f).

a.	To have a good relationship with	d.	To be really interested in
b.	To quickly become friends	e.	To be interested in the same things
c.	To be in a relationship with someone	f.	From that point to now

D. Focus on language

Read the comments in Activity B again. Discuss the questions with your partner.

1. What tense do the speakers use to talk about when they first met?
2. What tense do the speakers use to talk about the length of their relationship?
3. What verb do the speakers use to talk about the future meeting of the person and the listener?

ISBN: 978-3-12-501689-7

Lesson 1: Talking about friends – intermediate (B1) level

E. Preparing to speak

One of your friends is coming to visit you at your school. In Activity F, you're going to tell your partner about them. Before you speak, make some notes to plan what you will say. Don't write full sentences!

Notes

How will you describe your friend?

How will you describe how you met?

How will you talk about the length of your relationship?

How will you predict how your partner and your friend will get on?

F. Speaking

Work in pairs. Take it in turns to speak about your friends.

1. Speaker A, tell Speaker B about your friend. Speaker B, would you like to meet Speaker A's friend?
2. Speaker B, tell Speaker A about your friend. Speaker A, would you like to meet Speaker B's friend?

G. How did you do?

Work in pairs. Think about the speaking you did in Activity F. Discuss these questions. Use the success criteria to help you.

1. How successful were you?
2. Did you use the language you planned to use?
3. What will you do better next time?

Telling someone about your friend successfully means:

☐ Using the past simple to describe how you met.
☐ Using relationship vocabulary to describe your relationship.
☐ Using adjectives to describe your friend.
☐ Using the present perfect to describe the length of your relationship.
☐ Using 'will' or 'be going to' to predict how people will get on.

ISBN: 978-3-12-501689-7

Lesson 2: Spoken film reviews – pre-intermediate (A2/B1) level

Today we are going to:

- Talk about films we have seen recently.
- Listen to a spoken review of a film.
- Learn to organise a spoken review.
- Revise vocabulary to talk about films.

So that you can:

- Chat to others about films you have seen.

A. Introduction

Work in pairs. Discuss these questions together.

1. What was the last film you saw?
2. What did you think of it?
3. What can you remember about the story and the actors?
4. What is your favourite film? Why?

B. Make your choice

Today, you're going to give a spoken review of a film you have seen.

Choose a film. Make notes about it in the box. Include the name of the film, the actors, the characters and the story. You can use the internet to help you.

Notes

C. Listening

Listen to Jenna giving a spoken review of a film she saw at the weekend. Answer the questions.

1. What film did she see?
2. What did she think of it?
3. Does she think Tomoko should go to see it?

ISBN: 978-3-12-501689-7

Lesson 2: Spoken film reviews – pre-intermediate (A2/B1) level

D. Vocabulary focus

Match the words and phrases (1-8) to their meanings (A-H). You can use your dictionary to help you.

Example: 1. B

1	A rom-com	A	The story happens in [a country, city, year].
2	A sci-fi film	B	A romantic comedy film.
3	It's set in…	C	The story is from [a book, a true event]
4	It's based on…	D	I think you'll like it. You should watch it.
5	You should check it out.	E	A science fiction film (e.g. about space, robots or aliens)
6	I don't think it's for you.	F	The film was made in [a city, country, year]
7	It's about…	G	The story is…
8	It was filmed in…	H	I don't think you'll like it.

E. Spoken reviews

Read Jenna's review. Organise the sections of a spoken review in the correct order from 1-4.

I saw an amazing film the other day. It's called Into the West. It's set in Ireland in the '90s. It's about two brothers from Dublin. They have a horse but someone steals it and they try to find it. It was hilarious but also really moving. You should definitely check it out. You would love it.

How to organise a spoken film review

☐ Your recommendation

☐ Information about the film (e.g. story and characters)

☐ Your opinion of the film

☐ A short introduction

F. Practice

You're going to tell your partner about the film you chose in Activity B. Make some notes to prepare your spoken review below.

Notes

ISBN: 978-3-12-501689-7

Lesson 3: Talking about your plans – pre-intermediate (A2/B1)

A. Lesson aims & objective

Today we are going to:
- Learn vocabulary to talk about holidays / travel.
- Learn to ask about plans (using present continuous).
- Learn to talk about fixed plans (using present continuous).
- Learn to talk about possible plans (using 'might').
- Learn to respond to plans.

So that you can:
- Talk about your plans (e.g. for summer).

Discussion:

Work in pairs. Discuss the questions together.

1. Where did you go for your last holiday?
2. What did you do there?
3. Look at the aims to the left ('Today we are going to…'). Which will be:

a. New to you?

b. Revision for you?

4. Look at the objective to the left ('So that you can…'. How will this help you in your life outside class?

B. Learn by reading

Read three holiday plans below. Which holiday would you like to go on most? Why?

Jenna

I'm visiting my brother in Valencia this summer. I can't wait. The food there is incredible. I might go to Madrid for a weekend too.

So Young

I'm going to Ireland with my family next week. I hope the weather is nice. If it's nice, we might go hiking in the countryside. It's beautiful there.

Francois

I'm taking a train across Europe with my best friend this summer. We're going to Paris first, then Amsterdam, and finally Brussels. If we have time, we might go to Luxembourg. I can't wait to go shopping in Paris.

C. Focus on vocabulary

Use the comments in Activity B. to answer the questions below.

1. What holiday activities do they mention?
2. How do they say 'I'm very excited'?
3. How do they say 'very good'?

ISBN: 978-3-12-501689-7

Lesson 3: Talking about your plans – pre-intermediate (A2/B1)

D. Focus on language

Read the examples from Activity B. Discuss the questions with your partner.

I'm visiting my brother in Valencia this summer.

1) Is this a fixed plan or a possible plan?
2) Why do you think this?
3) What tense do they use for this plan?

If we have time, we might go to Luxembourg.

1) Is this a fixed plan or a possible plan?
2) Why do you think this?
3) What language point do they use for this plan?

E. Keeping a conversation going

Match the responses below to the three comments in Exercise B.

1. Oh, that sounds like fun. I'm not a huge fan of shopping but I would love to see Europe.
2. Oh wow! I love Spain. The food is so delicious.
3. Oh lovely. I really hope the weather is nice.

a. Jenna
b. So Young
c. Francois

Read the tip box below on responding to plans and then write your response to Jenna, So Young and Francois' holiday plans.

Speaking tip

It's important to keep conversations going and show interest. You can do this by responding to what people tell you. When responding to plans, you should react and then give a reason for your reaction.

Oh wow! = reaction

I love Spain. The food is so delicious. = reason for reaction

F. Practice

1. Before you tell your partner about your plans for the summer, write your success criteria.

   A successful conversation about summer plans:
   ☐
   ☐
   ☐
   ☐
2. Tell your partner about your plans for the summer.

Reflection

After your conversation, discuss the questions below with your partner.

1. How well did you achieve your chosen success criteria?
2. What will you do differently in your next conversation?

ISBN: 978-3-12-501689-7

Answer Key
for Part B

Chapter 1

Knowing your material

Activity	Reason(s)
A. Introduction	▶ To engage learners in the topic. ▶ To awaken any prior knowledge learners have on this topic. ▶ For the teacher to assess what related language learners can already use.
B. Learn by reading	▶ To give a successful model of the intended conversation of the lesson. ▶ To present the target language (relationship phrases, present simple, present perfect, *will* + infinitive) in context.
C. Focus on vocabulary	▶ To expand the learners' vocabulary on the topic of relationships. ▶ To give the learners vocabulary they can use in the final task of the lesson. ▶ To practise understanding the meaning of vocabulary from context.
D. Focus on language	▶ To draw the learners' attention to the grammatical structures they will need in the intended conversation. ▶ To revise the use of these structures. ▶ To practise analysing language in context.
E. Preparing to speak	▶ To give learners time to consider their answer. ▶ To encourage learners to use the target language.
F. Speaking	▶ To give learners practice using the target language in context.
G. How did you do?	▶ To give learners time to reflect on the lesson. ▶ To develop the learners' reflection and self-assessment skills.

Chapter 1

Ask yourself why

In these examples there is one that is most likely the reason, but the important point is that the Overt Teacher knows why they have chosen a particular activity. They know what they want learners to get out of the activity and therefore are able to discuss this with their learners.

Activity	Why
A. In the lesson, the learners are going to read an article on fast fashion. **The teacher begins the lesson with some discussion questions on fashion and shopping habits**.	The opening discussion questions in any lesson tend to introduce learners to the topic but are also **an important opportunity for the teacher to assess what learners know about the topic (1)**. They may also warm learners up (2) and get them speaking English (3) but these will not be the primary goals. Reasons for including an activity can be from both the learners' and the teacher's perspective.
B. Before they read the article, **the learners look at the picture and the headline and try to guess what the article will be about**.	Depending on the lesson, any of these could be the reason for the activity. However, most likely it is **to practise their prediction skills (1)**, as this is a skill learners can apply outside the classroom – it's a more specific reason than (2). On the other hand, (3) is too specific and can't be generalised to other areas easily. By knowing the aim, the teacher can communicate this to the learners, which will hopefully help them to feel more engaged with the activity.
C. After they read, the teacher sets the learners some gist reading questions. **They put them in pairs to check their answers** before looking at them together.	Over the years many learners have told us they think pairwork is just to get them speaking (1). In this situation, however, the teacher has most likely selected the activity **to let learners check their ideas before sharing (2)**, therefore giving them confidence and making them more likely to contribute. However, if a teacher pairs a weaker with a stronger learner or a new with an existing learner, they may want one to teach the other something (3). By knowing the reason, the teacher can ensure the conversation achieves the desired goal.
D. The learners are working on a vocabulary matching exercise based on the article. **The teacher stands up and walks from group to group monitoring.**	This very much depends on the teacher and the group in front of them. In an ideal world the learners are on task and **the teacher can assess problematic areas that need further discussion (3)**. While it's important to check learners are completing the right exercise (1), that should only be a brief part of monitoring. Making sure the learners are not using their phones (2) will depend on the exercise they are doing. Knowing why you are monitoring increases the chances of effective monitoring. Monitoring for the sake of monitoring might have a detrimental effect if learners are disturbed.

Chapter 1

Why did the writer write this sentence?

As Scott Thornbury mentions in his video blog on futurity (2012), the future continuous is 'very useful, very common but it's seldom taught as a future form'. It is often presented as an action in progress at a specific time in the future, but this doesn't really dig into its uses. In this example, the speaker is most likely introducing a request for a favour. In this situation the first housemate has mentioned the shops, so in their next message will most likely ask the second housemate to buy something for them.

Why did they do that? Using successful people as models

Possible aims might be:

Today we are going to:

- Learn vocabulary chunks to talk about global warming.
- Learn to use your body language to signal an interruption.
- Learn to agree / disagree politely.
- Learn to use your facial expressions to show agreement / disagreement.
- Learn to talk about consequences (using 1st and 2nd conditional).

So that you can:

- Have a discussion about global issues (e.g. global warming).

Discussing the learners' 'why'

Learner A

Working at a multinational company where English is the dominant language but is the second language of their colleagues, knowing fast speech is not necessarily going to help Learner A as it might make them less comprehensible to their colleagues. They may also feel that discussing their weekend plans is not relevant for them as they do not speak English with their friends outside work.

The teacher can point out that learning about fast speech is as much about recognising it when they hear it as producing it. Learner A does not have to produce fast speech themselves, but knowing that it exists will help them if they travel to English-speaking destinations for work. In addition, speaking about plans is very common at work and this language is transferrable from social to work environments.

Learner B

All of this lesson will be relevant for them. Pointing out how knowledge of fast speech can improve their comprehension if they're travelling in English-speaking countries could raise Learner B's engagement.

Learner C

Much like Learner A, Learner C might feel fast speech would be an impediment to communication with their Brazilian son-in-law. However, pointing out the usefulness of being able to recognise and understand it in movies and TV shows could help them to be more engaged in the lesson.

Chapter 2

Writing real-world objectives

a. This objective speaks directly to the learners ('you') and follows our suggested structure but is quite broad in its scope. If these learners are going to take the IELTS exam, it is relevant, but there is no guidance as to how exactly they will be better able to complete writing task 2.

b. By including 'the learners', this objective does not speak directly to the learners, but rather speaks about them in the third person. The focus of this objective is also grammar-based as opposed to containing a practical real-world application like 'complaining about poor service in a hotel'. It assumes a level of knowledge of particular grammatical terms ('negative inversion') that probably wouldn't exist at this level.

c. This objective speaks to the learners directly and gives them a real-life goal. It is written in learner-friendly language and is therefore easier for learners to understand and apply to their lives.

Writing decontextualised objectives

Contextualised objectives	Decontextualised objectives
Today we are going to: ▸ Skim read a forum about climate change. ▸ Learn to identify and analyse different arguments about climate change. ▸ Learn to critically assess the climate change arguments. ▸ Learn to share your opinion on climate change. **So that you can:** ▸ Analyse climate change arguments and discuss your opinion on climate change issues.	**Today we are going to:** ▸ Skim read a forum about climate change. ▸ Learn to identify and analyse different arguments. ▸ Learn to critically assess arguments. ▸ Learn to share your opinion on arguments we've read. **So that you can:** ▸ Analyse arguments on major issues and discuss your opinion of them (e.g. climate change issues).

While these aims and objectives both outline the same lesson, the first gives learners a single context in which they can apply what they've learnt outside the classroom, that of climate change issues. In the second example, learners can clearly see that climate change is just one situation in which they can apply what they've learnt. After this lesson, they can analyse arguments made about any major issue and share their opinion. By decontextualising the aims and objective, it can help learners see how the skills they are practising can be applied to other texts and situations, and help teachers to discuss this overtly with learners.

Writing effective aims

Though the aims may vary depending on the exact group of learners, their level and what input has come beforehand, at least some of these are likely to be included:

Today we are going to:
- Listen to spoken reviews of restaurants.
- Learn to organise a spoken review (introduction > comments > recommendation).
- Revise vocabulary to talk about restaurants / service.
- Revise adjectives to describe food.
- Learn to give recommendations using 'should'.

So that you can:
- Give a spoken review of a restaurant you visited (e.g. to a friend).

Chapter 2

Here is an assessment of the aims, answering the questions you will read in Try it out:

a. These aims are structured so it is clear that completing them will help the learners to achieve the lesson objective. They will be given clear models of their objective (a spoken review of a restaurant) and a structure to follow. They will revise or learn the language they need to achieve the objective.

b. There are clear signals in the study verbs about which sections will be new for them ('Listen', 'Learn') and which ones they are revisiting ('Revise'). See **Part A, Key principles 1, 2 and 3, 'Effective aims'** for more information about using study verbs.

c. There is an assumption that these pre-intermediate (A2/B1) learners have prior knowledge of vocabulary and adjectives for restaurants and food, so this will be revised rather than introduced in the lesson.

d. Examples of the organisation of a spoken review and the language for recommendations are given in brackets so it is clear to learners what they will be learning.

Formatting aims and objectives

Here are two possible formats for the aims and objective of this lesson.

Today we are going to: / In this lesson, we will:

- Talk about our friends.
- Read people's comments about their friends.
- Learn vocabulary for talking about our relationships.
- Revise how to talk about how we met someone (using the past simple).
- Revise how to describe the length of a relationship (using the present perfect).
- Revise how to predict how people will get on (using 'will' and 'be going to').

So that you can: / So that you are better able to:

- Describe your relationship with someone (e.g. before you introduce them to a friend).

We are learning to (WALT):

- Describe your relationship with someone (e.g. before you introduce them to a friend).

What I'm looking for (WILF):

- Using vocabulary for talking about relationships.
- Talking about how you met someone (using the past simple).
- Talking about the length of a relationship (using the present perfect).
- Predicting how people will get on (using 'will' and 'be going to').

The language is at intermediate (B1) level and the only metalanguage is the names of grammar points which we would expect these learners to be familiar with. The objective is clearly marked through the signpost 'So that you can', 'So that you are better able to' or 'We are learning to'. The aims are organised so that it is clear how each one leads into the next and builds towards the objective. In the first example, they mirror the order of activities on the worksheet so learners can clearly see how the lesson will unfold. In the second example, they provide possible success criteria so learners can see what will be expected of them. We examine success criteria in more depth in **Part B, Chapter 3**.

Chapter 2

Beginning the learning conversation

Here are some possible questions you could use to begin a conversation about the objective and aims with learners. They could be adapted depending on the level of the learners or even translated into your learners' language in the case of monolingual groups.

Question	Reflection
1. Which of these aims will be challenging for you?	This question helps learners to identify the areas of the lesson they will need to put most of their energy into. It helps you see who will need more support with each of the aims.
2. Which aim(s) are you already confident with?	This question helps learners to identify aims they will be revising or which might be less challenging for them. This can help you identify aims which you might not need to spend as much time on or to identify learners who can offer support to others who are weaker in this area.
3. What else do you think you need to learn to achieve this objective?	This helps learners to consider what they already know, what they will learn and what else they might need to know in order to achieve the objective, giving them some input and agency over what is being learnt in the lesson.
4. How will you use this objective in your real life?	This helps learners to see the personal relevance of this lesson. This can lead to them engaging more with the lesson as they see how it will help them. It can help you with future lesson planning as you learn more about your learners and how they see themselves using English outside the class.

Keeping the conversation going throughout the lesson

The aim of this activity is to ensure the learners have some of the language they will need to describe their film and make a recommendation in the final activity. There is an assumption that at pre-intermediate (A2/B1) level, learners will already be aware of some or even most of the language being presented. Stopping after Activity D and discussing the reason for the activity in relation to the lesson aims and objective and their own personalised goals means it is more likely that learners will not ignore any language they already think they know or wonder why the language level seems 'easy' to them.

Questions like these could help learners to have this conversation:

- What was the point of this activity?
- How will this language help you with your objective in this lesson?
- What other language do you know to describe films?
- Which language was new to you?
- Why do you think there was language that you already knew in this task?
- Which pieces of vocabulary do you want to include in the final task?

The final question is particularly useful when learners have worked with a range of lexis, skills or language points during the lesson. Not all of it will be new for them and some of it might not be hugely relevant for them. Allowing learners to decide which is most relevant and which they want to practise gives an element of personalisation as well as keeping them focused on the final objective. In this lesson, for example, the learners have already decided on the film they will speak about so are aware if they will need to use 'thriller', 'rom-com', 'sci-fi' or another word to describe it.

Chapter 3

Using aims and objectives to create success criteria

These are possible success criteria for this activity:

Telling an engaging story of a night out means:

- ☐ Introducing your story using 'You won't believe what happened last night.'
- ☐ Using your chosen vocabulary chunks to describe your activities.
- ☐ Beginning your story using a past continuous sentence to set the scene.
- ☐ Using past simple to describe the main actions of the story.
- ☐ Using past continuous to give background to the main actions and make the story more interesting.
- ☐ Using story linkers from the lesson so your story is easy to understand.
- ☐ Using a past perfect sentence to add background information to your story.

Notice how the success criteria closely mirror the aims and objective. The whole lesson builds up to a final communicative task of telling an engaging story, so each of the areas covered during the lesson should be a success factor in the final task. Here are a few points to note about these success criteria:

1. The objective of 'telling an engaging story' has moved from the bottom of the list of aims and objectives to the top of the criteria, focusing attention on this as the task.
2. The criteria may be worded slightly differently from the aims as by this point of the lesson, learners would have a more detailed understanding of that language point or skill. One example is 'Using story linkers from the lesson so your story is easy to understand'. In this criterion, the words 'easy to understand' have been added to what was presented in the aims. The assumption here is that in the lesson, the reason for using cohesive devices and not just the lexical items themselves has been examined. Learners therefore have a deeper understanding by the time the success criteria are discussed.
3. In a lesson covering 'activities on nights out', you would expect a wide range of lexis to be covered, not all of which will be relevant for every learner. For this reason, in the success criteria we can refer to vocabulary sections in the lesson and allow learners to choose which vocabulary chunks they will use in their own personal success criteria.

Chapter 3

Using a successful model to create success criteria

Below are possible success criteria based on this model. Of course, they may vary depending on the exact ability of the A2 group and what is covered in the lesson.

When you introduce a friend to one of your classmates, you should:

- ☐ Begin with 'This is…' and their name.
- ☐ Tell your classmate about the relationship (e.g. 'She is my sister / best friend.')
- ☐ Use the past simple to talk about when you met.
- ☐ Tell your classmate about their job.
- ☐ Use 'a' or 'an' before the job.
- ☐ Tell your classmate what your friend likes doing.
- ☐ Use 'verb + *-ing*' after 'like' or 'love'.

Writing unsuccessful models

Here is an example of an unsuccessful formal email requesting information.

Jerry Flynn **Send**

To **cc bcc**

Subject

Heya,

How's it going? I looked at your website and I was hoping to get some more info on your tours to Glendalough. Can you tell me when the next tours are as soon as you know? Also, does the tour include hotels and breakfast? Can you tell me more about this? Thanks so much.

Cheers,
Jerry Flynn

The purpose of the email has been retained in that the information being requested is the same. However, the elements from the lesson that create success have been removed, as follows:

- There are no longer clear paragraph breaks.
- All questions are in a single paragraph, rather than having one question per paragraph.
- There are no formal phrases to open and close the email.
- There are no formal phrases to introduce the information requests

Chapter 3

Using an unsuccessful model to create success criteria

These questions would help learners to discuss the model and decide how successful it is.

Work in pairs. Read the email. Discuss the questions.

1. Do you think the reader (Ms Molloy) will give the writer (Jerry Flynn) the information they want?
2. Is the email formal or informal? How can you tell?
3. How many paragraphs are there? What information is in each paragraph?
4. How could you organise it differently to help the reader to understand it?

Through that discussion success criteria similar to these can be negotiated:

A successful email to request information:
- ☐ Has paragraphs.
- ☐ Starts a new paragraph for each question.
- ☐ Uses formal phrases to open and close the email.
- ☐ Uses formal phrases to introduce the information requests.

Choosing success

Here are examples of what success could look like for each of these learners:

Learner A (elementary, A2)	Learner B (average pre-intermediate, A2/B1)	Learner C (high pre-intermediate, A2/B1)
Successfully having a conversation about someone's outfit means: ☐ Beginning with a compliment. ☐ Using 2 of the clothing words / phrases from the lesson. ☐ Telling the story of the outfit using past simple.	Successfully having a conversation about someone's outfit means: ☐ Beginning with a compliment. ☐ Using 4 of the clothing words/ phrases from the lesson. ☐ Asking your partner a question about their outfit using past simple questions. ☐ Telling the story of the outfit using past simple.	Successfully having a conversation about someone's outfit means: ☐ Beginning with a compliment. ☐ Using 5 of the clothing words/ phrases from the lesson. ☐ Asking your partner a question about their outfit using past simple questions. ☐ Using the fast speech pronunciation of 'did you'. ☐ Telling the story of the outfit using past simple.

It is important to remember that these are just possible examples of what success could look like for these learner profiles. While level is an important factor in selecting success criteria, so too are learner needs. For example, a stronger learner might decide fast speech is not relevant for them. They may be working in an international context in which fast speech might make the learner less intelligible to their colleagues. In this case, the learner may choose to avoid it altogether.

Chapter 3

Visualising success

Here are possible success criteria for each level, with later levels adding to earlier levels:

At this level…	The foundations 	The rooms 	The roof 	The finished house 
…the review:	☐ Tells the story of the film. ☐ Uses vocabulary from the lesson to talk about the film.	☐ Follows the structure of a spoken review. ☐ Introduces the review with the past simple.	☐ Tells the story of the film in present simple.	☐ Gives a recommendation (using 'You would love it!' / 'You should check it out!')

Chapter 4

Reflecting on success

Each of the criteria allows for possible layers of success. Here are possible reflection questions for these criteria:

A successful discussion about big issues in the news means:

- ☐ **Using an introductory phrase in the past simple to introduce a big issue you read**
  - ☐ Did I use an introductory phrase?
  - ☐ What phrase was it?
  - ☐ Was it in the past simple?
- ☐ **Using a range of collocations to describe big issues**
  - ☐ Which collocations from the lesson did I use?
- ☐ **Keeping the conversation going by commenting on what people say**
  - ☐ Did I keep the conversation going?
  - ☐ How did I do it?
  - ☐ When did I comment on what people said? What did I say about it?
- ☐ **Showing interest / surprise with phrases and intonation**
  - ☐ Did I show interest when my partner was speaking?
  - ☐ When and how did I show interest?
  - ☐ What phrases did I use?
  - ☐ When did I use intonation?

Setting up effective peer-to-peer feedback

Give learners clear success criteria to refer to so they can connect their feedback to specific points.

To talk about your plans, you should:

- ☐ Use 'I am going to' if you know the places and times.
- ☐ Use 'I will' if you decide your plan now.
- ☐ Use a verb without 'to' after 'I will' and 'I am going to'.

Provide sentence prompts to help the learners to give this feedback. For example:

- 'I think that is correct because you used…'
- 'I don't think that is correct because you used…'
- 'You use 'I will' if you decide your plan now.'
- 'You use 'I am going to' if you have places and times.'

Both success criteria and sentence prompts ensure that learners give each other the correct information and that it is constructive.

Monolingual learners may prefer to use their first language, but would still benefit from sentence prompts in their own language to ensure that the discussion is supportive.

Chapter 4

Setting up effective repetition

Effective repetition relies on the learners knowing what they are going to do and why they are doing it. Following these steps will ensure learners can notice their progress each time they tell their story:

1. Before learners tell their story, they decide on their personal success criteria.
2. Learners stand up and find a partner. They tell each other their stories.
3. The teacher claps their hand to signal the end of the first stage of storytelling.
4. Learners look at their personal success criteria. They decide which ones they have already met, and which they need to continue to work on. If they have met them all, they select an extra criterion to work on.
5. The teacher gives feedback to learners on what they did well, any common errors and any specific issues based on personal success criteria.
6. Learners find a new partner and tell their story again.
7. After each retelling, learners reflect on their personal success criteria and the teacher gives feedback and helps the learners to develop their stories.
8. At the end of the storytelling, learners reflect on their overall progress. The teacher gives any final whole-class feedback.

Making homework meaningful

One possible homework task for this lesson would be for learners to plan a spoken review and to record it on their phones. Learners can then self-assess and re-record as many times as they want to. They might then submit the recording to you, tell another learner in the class their spoken review, or tell someone outside the class. In future lessons, you can include follow-up discussions on the learners' experience and success to help them notice their progress. This task relies on leaners being able to listen back and self-assess what they have done so overt discussions in the lesson around success criteria are probably also necessary.

To help learners prepare for this task, you could set the following discussion questions in groups:

1. What feedback did you receive on your spoken reviews today?
2. Based on that feedback, what do you want to improve upon in your homework task?
3. What language and skills from the lesson will you need to make this improvement?

Setting up effective post-lesson repetition

The instructions include the steps learners must carry out to achieve success in this activity. However, it does not lay out exactly who should work together, how they should contact each other or when and how they should submit their work. While these might not seem like big hurdles, without detailing this information, we are placing unnecessary obstacles in front of the learners. By adding in an extra section, we can remove these problems and make it more likely that learners will be able to complete the work.

This section should include:
- Space for learners to write in the names of their partners.
- How / when exactly they should contact each other (e.g. on Teams, on your schools system, immediately after class, in a study session, etc.)
- How and when they should submit what they produce.

Chapter 4

The final instructions would therefore look like this:

Instructions

You are going to discuss TV shows you like / dislike with your partners.

1. Prepare a list of TV shows you like / dislike.
2. Contact your partners using our WhatsApp group. (My partners are ___________)
3. Record the conversation of you discussing your list with your partners.
4. Listen back to your conversation and use the success criteria to assess it.
5. Record it again if you are not satisfied.
6. Email your audio recording to the teacher for feedback by Monday 17 October.

Post-lesson outcome mining

While each of the possible tangents are interesting and perhaps all worthy of discussion at some point, only situation 3 is a valuable addition to this particular lesson. This learner sharing their experience and their knowledge could be a wonderful opportunity for the other learners. Their tips can become part of the success criteria and learners can choose which tips they will apply in their own presentations. While using body language in presentations was not one of the initial lesson aims, when reflecting on what has been learnt at the end of the lesson it would definitely be worth discussing and encouraging learners to apply to their own lives outside the classroom.

On the other hand, situations 1 and 2 do not add to the current lesson. Situation 1 could be dealt with by a quick aside answering their question either immediately or a little later while other learners are working on something else. Situation 2, however, is a potential derailment of the lesson. It might be interesting and useful to your learners but would move your lesson away from the objective as opposed to adding to it. In this case, tell the learners that you will make a note of what they said, and aim to come back to it in a future lesson.

Chapter 5

A successful skills development lesson

This would be an unsuccessful skills development lesson because while the learners practise the sub-skill, they do not overtly discuss it and therefore do not develop their knowledge of the sub-skill. They do not receive input on it or a written record about it. In the final stage of the lesson learners discuss the topic, but not the skill and how it could be applied to other areas in their lives. The only feedback learners receive is about the answers to the gist questions at the beginning of the lesson and their use of vocabulary in the final discussion.

By adding stages in which overt discussion takes place, the lesson can be changed to lead to much clearer development of the sub-skill. For example:

- Learners talk about the topic of the article.
- They try to gist read the first half of the article in 1 minute.
- They discuss how much of the article they read and what their strategy was for gist reading.
- They learn a new strategy for gist reading (from the teacher or their classmates).
- They gist read the second half of the article for 1 minute using the new strategy.
- They discuss how well the strategy worked for them and receive feedback from the teacher.
- They learn vocabulary from the article related to the topic.
- They speak about the topic using the vocabulary.
- They receive feedback on their use of the vocabulary.
- They reflect on the lesson objective and discuss when they might gist read for interest in their lives outside the classroom.

Talking about listening

Here are a few ideas for questions and the kinds of responses you might expect for questions before the task.

Questions	Possible responses from learners
What do you think will be challenging about this listening text?	1. It is a radio show so we can't see their faces. 2. They might make references to things we don't know about the topic. 3. They might have accents we don't understand. 4. They might speak too quickly to understand.
What strategies can you use to make it less challenging?	1. We can listen to the speakers' intonation to help us understand how they feel. 2. If they make references we don't understand, we can ignore them and focus on what we know. Maybe we can ask others about these references later. We're learning English, not climate issues, and we can't know everything. 3. Maybe we could think about what they might say before listening so we are ready. 4. We can listen for the key words we've already learnt and use them to help us if they're speaking quickly.

For questions asked after the task, the responses would very much depend on what occurred during the task, and are therefore more challenging to predict. Listening to the audio yourself should help you to see what the learners might have problems with.

Chapter 5

Questions	Possible responses from learners
Was the listening challenging in the way you expected? How did it challenge you?	1. Yes. They spoke very quickly so sometimes it was hard to follow. It made me feel a bit nervous. 2. Yes but also, there was some noise outside the window. This made it more difficult to hear.
What strategies did you use to make it less challenging? Did they help? What could you do differently next time?	1. When I got lost, I tried to listen out for key words that we learnt in the lesson. I thought about what we predicted. I tried to ignore what I didn't know and focus on what I know. I was able to understand the basic ideas. 2. I could not focus so I stopped listening. I forgot to focus on key words. Next time I will try to focus just on key words and ignore noise from outside. Sometimes there is noise in life.

Note that you might phrase the questions differently depending on the actual content and level of authenticity of the audio.

Talking about reading

The following questions would help to focus the learners on this sub-skill and encourage reflection on their approach to reading for gist in both their L1 and English.

1. Why is reading for gist important?
2. When might you use it in your real life?
3. What strategies do you have for this sub-skill?
4. Do you already do this in your language? When? Why? / Why not?
5. Do you already do this in English? When? Why? / Why not?
6. How can you practise this skill outside the classroom?

Here are possible responses from pre-intermediate (A2/B1) learners:

1. We can read a text quickly. We don't need to spend a lot of time reading every word.
2. When I get an email from my school / work.
3. I do not read every word. I do not put my finger on the page/screen to follow each word. I let my eyes fall across the page. I only read information words like nouns, verbs and adjectives.
4. I do this every day in my language. I never read emails in detail.
5. In English I usually read every word because I am worried that I will not understand something.
6. I will read emails from the school quickly, and then in more detail to check I understood.

Chapter 5

Discussing comprehension

Here are some sample questions which would both reveal comprehension and mirror what learners might do after reading a short story outside the classroom.

1. Tell your partner what the story was about.
2. What did you like / dislike about the story?
3. What questions did you have after reading the story?
4. Which character did you sympathise with? Why?

Giving a written record of a skill

This gapfill is designed to encourage learners to think about the sub-skill and consider the various tips and descriptions, without being overly challenging linguistically. The level of challenge should be slightly below their level so as not to impede comprehension or consideration of the sub-skill itself.

Read the description of the sub-skill. Choose the correct word for each gap from the box. There is 1 extra word you don't need.

pause	type	stressed	signposting	key	final	contrasting	phrases	refocus

Sometimes when listening to a presentation, we can get a bit lost. Most speakers will use words and __________ to help you to understand their talk or __________ your attention if you get lost or lose concentration. This is called 'signposting'.

When listening to a presentation, remember:

- Signpost words are usually __________(spoken clearly).
- The speaker will usually __________after the signpost.
- Signposts will tell you the type of information coming next:
  - *However, / While / Although* = followed by __________information
  - *Importantly, / It's important to remember / Crucially* = followed by __________points
  - *Finally, / In conclusion,* = followed by __________points

You can use __________to help you understand where you are when listening to a presentation, so listen carefully for it.

Bibliography

Alexander, R., Hardman, F. and Hardman, J. with Rajab, T. and Longmore, M. (2017) 'Changing Talk, Changing Thinking: interim report from the in-house evaluation of the CPRT/UoY Dialogic Teaching Project' https://cprtrust.org.uk/wp-content/uploads/2017/07/Alexander-et-al-EEF-in-house-interim-report-final-170714.pdf

Black, P. and Wiliam, D. (1998) *Inside the Black Box: Raising standards through classroom assessment* Kings College London

Clarke, S. (n.d.) 'Formative Assessment: a summary' https://www.shirleyclarke-education.org/what-is-formative-assessment/

De Chazal, E. (2014) *English for Academic Purposes* Oxford University Press

Gerzon, N. (n.d.) 'Communicating Learning Goals and Success Criteria with Students' https://csaa.wested.org/wp-content/uploads/2020/10/Communciating-Learning-Goals-and-Success-Criteria-with-Students.pdf

Glew-O'Leary, J. and Pepper, M. (2021) 'An Action Research Report: On VR in The Hybrid Classroom', IH Manchester

Hattie, J. (2008) *Visible Learning: A Synthesis of Over 800 Meta-Analyses Relating to Achievement* Routledge

Hattie, J. (2012) *Visible Learning for Teachers: Maximising Impact on Learning* Routledge

Hattie, J. and Clarke, S. (2019) *Visible Learning Feedback* Routledge

Hattie, J. and Zierer, K (2018) *10 Mindframes for Visible Learning.* Routledge

Mavridi, S. (2020) 'The hybrid classroom. Dilemmas, choices and solutions' https://www.teachingenglish.org.uk/news-and-events/world-teachers-day/2020/hybrid-classroom-dilemmas-choices-and-solutions

Mercer, S. and Dörnyei (2020) *Engaging Language Learners in Contemporary Classrooms* Cambridge University Press

Norrington-Davies , D. (2016) *Teaching Grammar: From Rules to Reasons* Pavilion ELT

Nunan, D (2011) *Teaching English to Young Learners* Anaheim University Press

Nuthall, G.A. (2007) *The Hidden Lives of Learners.* Wellington: New Zealand Council for Educational Research

Plews, M. (2015) 'Idea 181: 'Chilli Challenge' Differentiation Approach' http://www.bigblogofteachingideas.com/mathematics-2/idea-181-chilli-challenge-differentiation-approach/

Richards, J. and Renandya, W.A. (2002), *Methodology in Language Teaching An Anthology of Current Practice* Cambridge University Press

Scott, T. and Tann, K. (2021) *Bridging disciplinary knowledge: the challenge of integrating EAP in business education*

Scrivener, J. (2011) *Learning Teaching: The Essential Guide to English Language Teaching, Third Edition* Macmillan

Scrivener, J. (2014) 'Demand-high teaching' The European Journal of Applied Linguistics and TEFL, 3(2), 47-58.

TEFL Training Institute Podcast (2021) 'Teacher supervision without observation (with Mario Rinvolucri) https://www.tefltraininginstitute.com/podcast/2019/9/3/teacher-supervision-without-observation-with-mario-rinvolucri

Thornbury, S. (2011) 'A is for Aims' https://scottthornbury.wordpress.com/2011/04/24/a-is-for-aims/

Thornbury, S. (2012) 'F is for Futurity' https://scottthornbury.wordpress.com/2012/03/04/f-is-for-futurity/

Thrasher, T. (2022) *Avatar psychology: The impact of avatar representation on language learning* https://www.researchgate.net/publication/359929211_Avatar_psychology_The_impact_of_avatar_representation_on_language_learning

Tishauser, J. (2019) 'Graham Nuthall: Educational research at its best' https://researched.org.uk/2019/02/26/graham-nuthall-educational-research-at-its-best/

Ur, P. (1996) *A course in language teaching* Cambridge University Press

From the editor

Overt Teaching is a call to action for teachers, showing us how to put learners at the centre of discussions about learning. By doing this, we can keep them engaged and motivated about what is happening in their lessons and help them to see how it connects to their lives beyond the classroom.

In the book, **David Byrne** and **Mark Heffernan** show how the Overt Teacher:

- Understands why they are doing each activity in the classroom;
- Communicates this clearly to learners;
- Connects what happens in the classroom to what happens beyond it;
- Helps learners to understand what success looks like;
- Teaches learners to notice their progress and reflect on how to improve.

A	**Part A** starts with some theory, showing how Overt Teaching can be purposeful and effective for both teachers and learners. It examines where Covert Teaching might come from, and the arguments for becoming a more Overt Teacher. It then presents five Principles of Overt Teaching which are built on in the rest of the book.
B	**Part B** provides a series of Tips and Tasks to help you make the move towards more Overt Teaching. There are also ideas to help you Try it out and Take it further, ensuring that your learners really do become the centre of their own learning discussions.
C	**Part C** examines how the Principles of Overt Teaching might be relevant across a range of teaching contexts and modes of online delivery. It also looks at how to apply the principles to materials writing and teacher development. Each section includes practical examples of how the principles of Overt Teaching can be put into action.

The ideas and techniques presented in ***Overt Teaching*** are tried and tested. David and Mark have been using them in their own classrooms and training others to use them for a number of years, receiving positive feedback from teachers and learners alike. Now they're ready to share them with you and your learners. Throughout the editing process, David and Mark have already changed how I think about communicating aims, objectives and success to my learners, and I hope the same will be true for you once you've read the book yourself.

Sandy Millin

Images:
back cover David Byrne; **front cover** 123RF.com (Marcin Chodorowski), Nidderau; **10, various** 123RF.com (Dmytro Kozyrskyi); **11, various** 123RF.com (akhmad sobahus); **18, various** 123RF.com (Inna Kharlamova); **64** 123RF.com (bigmouse); **95** 123RF.com (fad82); **113** 123RF.com (denvitruk); **114** 123RF.com (Aynur Sadigova); **115.1** 123RF.com (Daniel Ernst); **115.2** 123RF.com (liza5450); **115.3** 123RF.com (sylv1rob1); **115.4** 123RF.com (Petro Bevz)

Text credits:
10, 14, 15, 16, 24, 25, 28, 29 Copyright © 2017 From 10 Mindframes for Visible Learning: Teaching for Success by John Hattie and Klaus Zierer. Reproduced by permission of Taylor and Francis Group, LLC, a division of Informa plc.; **14, 17** Copyright © 2012 From Visible learning for teachers: maximizing impact on learning by John Hattie. Reproduced by permission of Taylor and Francis Group, LLC, a division of Informa plc.; **19, 26, 27, 28, 30, 34, 51** Copyright © 2018 From Visible Learning: Feedback by Shirley Clarke and John Zierer. Reproduced by permission of Taylor and Francis Group, LLC, a division of Informa plc.; **81** © Life in the Countryside . . . the origins of Textploitation, https://textploitationtefl.com, 2015, **107** © Teacher Supervision Without Observation (With Mario Rinvolucri), TEFL Training Institute Podcast, 2021